# The Mustang

David Newhardt

MBI Publishing Company

This edition published in 2002 by MBI Publishing Company, Galtier Plaza, Suite 200, 380 Jackson Street, St. Paul, MN 55101-3885 USA

MBI Publishing Company books are also available at discounts in bulk quantity for industrial or sales-promotional use. For details write to Special Sales Manager at Motorbooks International Wholesalers & Distributors, Galtier Plaza, Suite 200, 380 Jackson Street, St. Paul, MN 55101-3885 USA.

Library of Congress Cataloging-in-Publication Data Available

ISBN 0-7603-1389-X

Printed in China

CONTENTS

# ACKNOWLEDGMENTS

Automotive books are, by their very nature, a team effort. The author can write the text, and the photographer can point the camera in the direction of the vehicles, but without the help of the automobiles owners and the input from the experts, the effort would be for nothing. It is with a warm thank you to these individuals who made their cars available for me to photograph: Bruce Meyer, Jay Lincoln, Scott Mead, John Lock, Kenn Funk, Monroe Weathers, Duane McKinnon, Bob Fria, Steve Grant, Jim Wahl, Luis A. Chanes, Kenny Maisano, Brian Sbardelli, Laurence A. Viole, Bob King, Mike Venarde, Sandra Landry, and Shannon Venarde. To my true friend Randy Leffingwell, thank you so much for the loan of the wonderful images. Having people knowledgeable in the field makes an author's life bearable. I owe a large debt of gratitude to these individuals: Bill Puck, Jon Schultz, Matt Stone, and Jim Dvorak. Many thanks to Ford's West Coast fleet goddess, Sandra Badgett. Doug Stokes and the gang at Irwindale Speedway: you're the best. Oh, to my long-time editor, Paul Johnson, thank you for your light touch. And a tip of the hat to all of the owners of the original pony car.

Every once in a while, Detroit produces a vehicle that hits the right button at the right time. Through a combination of superior styling, improved engineering, market conditions, good luck, or maybe the position of the planets, sometimes a vehicle rolls out of the plant and into American's heart.

Such an event took place on April 15, 1964, when the Ford Motor Company released its new Mustang, a personal car that offered sporty looks, performance, and attitude. And all of it was offered at an incredibly affordable price. What was Ford thinking? That maybe it could recoup some of the money spent on developing the Falcon. Using as many parts as possible from that popular economy car would help spread the immense costs incurred during development and production of a new car. If another vehicle could amortize tooling costs, profits would roll in that much sooner.

The original pony car changed the American automotive landscape forever. Although the Pontiac GTO is recognized as the first musclecar, Ford sold 500,000 Mustangs in its first year. After that first year's raging success, the high-performance youth market could no longer be ignored. Chrysler and General Motors jumped on the bandwagon and developed their own pony cars. Eventually, the competition created the glorious musclecar era. Since 1964, Ford has had a Mustang on top or near the top of the high-performance heap. The long list of legendary high-performance cars includes the Shelby GT350, the Boss 302, the Mustang SVO, and the Cobra R, just to name a few. This book is a celebration of Ford's greatest high-performance Mustangs.

## CHAPTER ONE

## THE PONYCAR THAT SPARKED A REVOLUTION

From humble beginnings, the mighty Mustang was born. As engineer Bob Negstad recounted, it was created "from floor sweeping." Ford planning manager Hal Sperlich teamed with Ford division boss Lee Iacocca to use the Falcon as a starting point. As Iacocca put it, it was a car that "you could drive to the country club on Friday night, to the drag strip on Saturday, and to church on Sunday."

With the unibody Falcon as the platform, Eugene Boridinat, Ford's styling director, organized an internal Ford styling competition. The winning entry, penned by David Ash and Joe Oros, was called the Mustang. It continued the Ford trend of naming vehicles after animals, such as the Thunderbird and Falcon. Base price was only $2,320.96, a price

Built on April 20, 1964, this Mustang Pace Car replica is one of only 190 made to commemorate the 48th annual Indianapolis 500-mile race. The release of the car was accompanied by a well-planned media blitz. By the end of production year 1965, Ford had sold more than 600,000 hardtop, fastback, and convertible Mustangs. Note how the factory stripe ended at the end of the hood and did not run under the bumper.

All 190 pace cars were fitted with the 260-ci V-8 rated at 164 horsepower. It was a sprightly performer and was the start of a long line of impressive small blocks. Note the generator that was installed on 1964-1/2 vehicles; alternators were installed in the 1965 model year.

virtually anyone visiting a showroom could justify. Mustang "Job One" rolled off the assembly line only 571 days after the prototype got the green light. At the time, no one could have imagined the success it would achieve or its far reaching impact on the automotive landscape.

## THE 1964-1/2 INDY PACE CAR COUPE

It was a perfect day in May in Indiana, the kind that the local chamber of commerce waxes poetic about in vacation literature. A race was being held in the state capital, the kind of race that the world waxes poetic about. And pacing the "Greatest Spectacle in Racing" was an automobile that the motoring press was waxing poetic about, an automobile that captured the enthusiasm of the times–the Ford Mustang.

Production was going full steam, yet the backlog of orders grew. Master marketer Lee Iacocca wanted to increase the new cars' profile even more. When Ford made the decision to use the Mustang as the pace car for the 1964 running

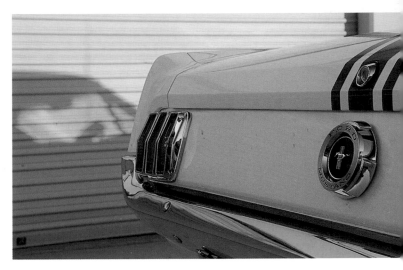

Ford used red-white-and-blue vertical bars with the horse emblem, so onlookers would know that this is an American horse, not a foreign one. The lavish use of brightwork in the interior was a common 1960s styling touch. The simulated holes on the spokes of the steering wheel were meant to evoke a sports car feel.

The first-year Mustang established the short trunk lid and long-hood pony car tradition. The center filler for the fuel tank stayed in the center of the rear panel for many years. Three vertical taillights continue to be a Mustang trademark. The stripe ended at the rear of the vehicle at the same position as on the nose.

of the 48th annual Indianapolis 500-mile race, Ford found itself in an enviable position, but it couldn't afford to specially produce the 38 convertible Mustangs needed for pace car duties. Every vehicle made was being rushed to buyers. So Ford went to its local Indianapolis dealerships and "procured" the needed cars.

All 38 pace cars were fitted with 289-ci V-8 engines, the largest V-8 in the lineup. Three Mustangs were set up for actual pacing duties, featuring the "Hi-Po" 271-horsepower 289-ci K-code engine and Borg-Warner four-speed. An increased capacity oil pan and radiator were part of the package. The cars were fitted with a heavy-duty suspension and Koni shocks to cope with the high speeds. The other 35 pace cars were in essence festival cars. A stock D-code

289-ci V-8, producing 210-horsepower, resided under the cars' hoods. A four-barrel carburetor and either a four-speed manual or an automatic transmission was also part of the package. The interior was red, white, or blue vinyl. All 38 Pace Car Mustangs were painted Wimbledon White, paint code M, and had pace car graphics and blue racing stripes.

To honor the Mustang's role and to increase public awareness, approximately 190 Mustang

**Following pages**
With the introduction of the GT option in 1965, performance took a big leap forward. A tiny emblem on the front fender told spectators that the potent K-code 289-ci engine was under the long hood. The high-revving engine produced 271 horsepower at 6,000 rpms.

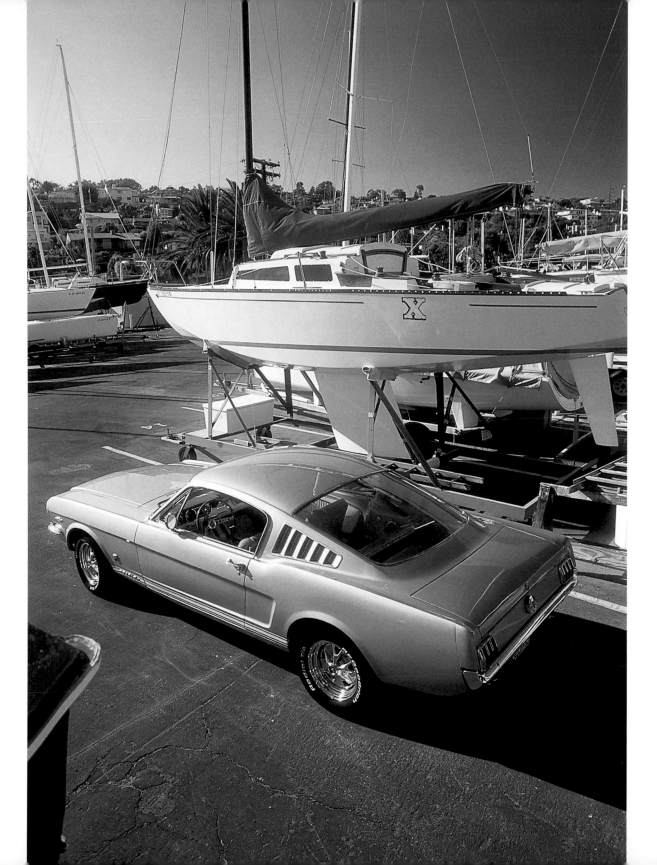

**Left**

The fastback model provided a great blend of a graceful form and function. The classic lines and tasteful styling made automotive history and influenced car design in the years that followed. The folding rear seat gave an impressive amount of storage room, and the large rear window flooded the interior with light.

**Below**

These extractor vents on the C-pillars were functional, helping to pull air out of the passenger space. For 1965 the rectangular speedometer was replaced by the round dial speedo, which better supported the performance car aura. The rim of this steering wheel is made of real wood.

pace car replica coupes were built in April and early May 1964. Ford ran a "Checkered Flag" sales contest among its dealerships; the winners were awarded a pace car replica. Unlike the actual pace cars, the coupes were painted Pace Car White, paint code C, and all of them had the same mechanicals. An F-code 260-ci V-8 engine carried a two-barrel C40F-9510-B carburetor. It produced 164-horsepower at 4,400 rpm, and torque came in at 258 foot-pounds at 2,200 rpm. Each replica was fitted with the three-speed Cruise-O-Matic automatic transmission, power steering, back-up lights, AM radio, and a white vinyl interior with blue accents. The sides were adorned with the same graphics enjoyed by the actual pace cars, and like all early Mustangs, the replicas differed from 1965 Mustangs in a number of areas. When the pace car replicas were rolling

15

With almost 1 horsepower per cubic inch, the 289 small-block V-8 quickly became a legendary engine. The quick-revving powerplant featured a 600 Autolite four-barrel carb, cast-aluminum pistons, and cast-iron block. With 271 horsepower on tap, it would match the performance of a Chevrolet 327.

Ford wanted a bona fide production race car to compete in SCCA (Sports Car Club of America) road racing. So Ford partnered with Carroll Shelby, and together they built one of the greatest sports cars of the 1960s—the 1965 Shelby GT350. The glamour the GT350 brought to the Mustang line was immeasurable, and the race car image as well as performance helped sell a lot of street cars.

16

To make the GT350 the best handling car possible, Shelby extensively modified the stock Mustang suspension. It featured lowered upper A-arms, large 1-inch roll bar, traction bars, and high-performance shocks. The small hood scoop was functional. The bumpers were largely decorative; most racers pulled them off before starting a race. The hood pin locks were necessary in holding the fiberglass hood down during the triple-digit speed excursions.

down the assembly line, a worker would write the words *PACE CAR* on top of the radiator support to identify the vehicle to other line workers.

Ford never officially built a 1964-1/2 model. Any Mustang built between March 1964 and August 17, 1964, is known as an early Mustang. About 150 items are unique to early Mustangs, such as the use of a generator, driver's footwell carpeting without a vinyl toe pad, and a nonadjustable passenger seat. Other features special to early Mustangs included smaller 4-1/2-inch fender emblems, seat belts anchored to the floor with eyebolts, and lower-pitched, larger horns. The Pace Car coupes were exactly like their production line brethren in regards to equipment fitment.

As the introductory year progressed, Ford ramped up production to satisfy the public's demand. The exposure gained at an Indy 500 on Memorial Day, 1964 only fueled the phenomenon that was to be the Mustang. Little did anyone know that the Mustang would become something of a regular at the famous 2.5-mile oval.

## THE 1965 GT CONVERTIBLE

From the early days of the automobile industry, manufacturers have known that the buying public would ask for more power, better handling, and the styling to set them apart. Mustang buyers wasted no time asking for more, and Ford was ready with more tempting treats. One of the first started with a *K*.

Ford had slipped its Hi-Po 289-ci engine into the Indy Pace Cars that actually saw high-speed

Built to compete at venues such as this, the 1965 GT350 was a justifiable legend in its own time. Notice how the racing stripes extend down to the bottom of the valence panel, unlike the Pace Car replicas built at the Ford factory.

The Shelby team took the already powerful 271-horsepower 289 and turned it into a voracious monster cranking out 306 horsepower at a lofty 6,000 rpm. The King Kong 289 featured ported and polished heads, custom-ground camshaft, Tri-Y headers, and a plethora of other high-performance parts. The car achieved 0 to 60 times under six seconds. Note that the circular rod connecting the inner fender wells was a device meant to stiffen the front suspension and improve handling.

duty on the track. The Hi-Po K code engine was the first high-performance step in the Mustang's long history. It became available to the public on April 17, 1965, and was just one component of Iacocca's "Total Performance." As part of the GT Equipment group, the 271-horsepower engine could fill the engine bay for $276.34. The small-block screamer could make the 6.95x14 Dual Red Band nylon tires lay down impressive black stripes. With its 10.5:1 compression ratio, premium fuel was mandatory. It developed 271 horsepower at 6,000 rpm and 312 foot-pounds at

The Shelby GT350 featured a well-appointed and purposeful interior with the requisite wood steering wheel and burly shifter. In order to save weight, rear seats were not installed. Wide competition seat belts gave a hint to the purpose behind the wheel. The large tachometer mounted atop the dash helped the driver monitor engine speed without taking the eyes too far off the road.

3,400 rpm. Topped with a 600-cubic feet per minute (cfm) Autolite four-barrel carburetor, the black painted iron block had a bore and stroke of 4.00 by 2.87 inches with slightly domed cast-aluminum pistons. Mechanical valve lifters with dual valve springs helped achieve the high engine speeds. The nodular cast-iron crankshaft, along with the 1-13/16-inch thick harmonic crankshaft balancer kept the engine in one piece. Threaded rocker arm studs, modified connecting rod bearings, caps and bolts, and a low restriction air filter helped produce power

The Shelby GT350H was the supercar built for the masses as well as for the Hertz Rent-A-Car company. This 1966 GT 350H lurks under a street light, waiting to take on the competition. The H model was a more humane version of the standard GT350, and the Hertz versions came with a back seat and a radio. One thousand were built and were rented to members of the Hertz Sports Car Club. Unfortunately, there is nothing like this at the airport rental lots nowadays.

on cue. Handling ignition was a mechanical-advance, dual-point distributor.

More power meant more demands on the suspension. The front long-arm/short-arm suspension was fitted with heavy-duty springs, raising the ride rate from 82 to 105 pounds per inch. The rear leaf springs were massaged as well, the ride rate increasing from 101 to 130 pounds per inch. The front stabilizer bar was beefed up from 0.69 to 0.84 inch. The result was a significantly firmer ride, and

The color of the full-length stripe on the Shelby GT350H was Bronze Metallic. Here it covers the functional hood scoop, which also provided clearance between the air cleaner and the hood.

Like its Ford cousin, the Shelby Mustang retained the timeless first-generation fastback lines. Ford established the long hood/short deck body theme that would be reflected in all the future pany and musclecars.

the 16:1 ratio steering (stock ratio was 19:1) made changing direction a more hurried evolution. The Hi-Po also had a heavy-duty rear end differential with a 9-inch rear axle ring, rather than the 8-inch unit installed in all other Mustangs.

The result of all this engineering work at Ford became clear on the road. In the October 1964 issue of *Car and Driver*, a 271-horsepower 289-ci V-8 Fastback Mustang was put through its paces. With a 4.11:1 rear axle ratio, the 'Stang hustled down the quarter mile in 14.0 seconds at 100 miles per hour and bolted from

0 to 60 in 5.2 seconds. Top speed was recorded at 112 miles per hour, and the front Kelsey-Hayes 10.0-inch ventilated disc brakes "passed our fade tests and simulated panic stops easily," the magazine said. In the pages of the September 1964 *Road & Track*, a 271-horse-power Mustang with a set of 3.89:1 gears clicked off 15.9 seconds at 85 miles per hour in the quarter-mile.

Behind the wheel, the GT driver saw a different view than that of standard Mustang owners. A five-instrument cluster featured a 140-mile-per-hour

The Magnum 500 was recognized as the factory Ford wheel to have. These durable wheels were made of steel and measured 14 by 6 inches. Surrounded by 6.95-by-14 Goodyear Blue Streak tires, the bias-ply tires were state of the art for the era.

speedometer in place of the regular Mustang 120-mile-per-hour unit. When the Interior Decor Group option was ordered for $107.08, two more gauges were installed—an 8,000-rpm tachometer and a clock. A full-length console was installed as well. More options allowed the buyer to equip the Mustang GT as close to country-club cruiser or racetrack terror as the buyer wanted.

By the end of the 1965 model year, 680,989 Mustangs had been built. Out of that lofty figure, only 7,232 were equipped with the K-code 289. While relatively rare, the $276.34 K-code option was a hell of a first step on the performance ladder.

### THE 1965 SHELBY GT350

Ford wanted to race the Mustang in Sports Car Club of America's (SCCA) production race car class, but Ford's efforts weren't successful. Lee Iacocca discussed the dilemma with former race car driver and team owner Carroll Shelby. Shelby said he could build the minimum number required and get busy winning in the B-Production class if Ford would make 100 Mustangs available to him quickly. Before he could say *race*, Shelby was working in a shop near Los Angeles International Airport putting together the package that would become the GT350.

Ford built the "knocked down" (incomplete) vehicles in two days at the San Jose, California, and shipped them to the Shelby hangars where the cars were completely outfitted. All of the cars were fastbacks with white exteriors and black interiors. Ironically, these hangars were some of the facilities used in the production of the North American P-51 Mustang fighter plane from World War II.

When the cars arrived, they were modified rather substantially, especially in the suspension department. The upper A-arms of the front suspension were lowered 1.0 inch, and the standard 0.625-inch antisway was replaced with a beefier 1.0-inch unit. The rear suspension was fitted with override traction bars, and Koni shock absorbers were installed on each corner. Standard Mustang front disc brakes were teamed with Fairlane station wagon 10-inch rear drums with sintered metallic competition pads.

The engine did not require extensive modifications. The small-block 289-ci V-8 proved to be strong and durable. Shelby wanted more than strong. He got it. An aluminum high-rise intake manifold and a 715-cfm Holley carburetor, part number S1MK-9510-A, were installed. This carb was fitted with a center pivot float that would not stick against the side of the float bowl under heavy cornering. The stock heads were removed, ported, and polished. Every reciprocating part was balanced. A custom-ground camshaft was installed, with 306-degree duration, .457-inch lift, and 78-degree overlap. A finned aluminum oil pan, holding 6.5 quarts, increased lubricating capacity. Exhaust gases were shown the door through Tri-Y tubular headers, routed through glass pack mufflers before exiting in front of the rear tires. After all the modifications were made, the 289 pumped out an incredible 306-horsepower at 6,000 rpm and 329 foot-pounds of torque at 4,200 rpm.

The gearbox was a cut-and-dried choice—an aluminum-case, Borg-Warner T-10 close-ratio four-speed. At the other end of the driveshaft lurked a Detroit Locker limited slip differential with 3.89:1 gears standard, but 4.11, 4.30, or 4.57 gears could be substituted. A set of 7.75x15-inch Goodyear Blue Dot tires, good for 130 miles per hour, provided traction. The stock steel hood was replaced with a fiberglass unit, complete with a functional hood scoop. The back seat was also removed and was replaced by a one-piece fiberglass shelf with a storage point for the spare tire.

About 200 pounds were shaved off the stock Mustang weight. Atop the dashboard went a Delco tachometer and an oil pressure gauge. The battery was installed in the trunk to balance the weight distribution for the first 325 vehicles, then it was moved to the engine compartment due to occasional fumes in the interior. Wide seat belts and a wooden steering wheel were some of the finishing touches. All of this sold for only $4,547!

The performance numbers tell the story. *Motor Trend* tested a GT350 in its May 1965 issue and ripped down the quarter-mile in 15.7 seconds at 91 miles per hour. The sports car rocketed from 0 to 60 miles per hour in 7.0 seconds, while stopping from the same speed took 140 feet.

And were the results worth the work? Trophies, trophies, as far as you could see.

Unlike the vents on the 1965 Shelby GT350, the 1966 model used a Plexiglas window installed in C-pillars to help overcome the large blind spot. The crisp lines of the Mustang design are seen here, the roof gracefully flowing into the deck surface.

## THE 1966 SHELBY GT350H

Only in America are dreams for rent. To think you could get off an airline flight and slip behind the wheel of a race car. The Hertz rental car company introduced a legion of drivers to the Shelby firm. In the short term it probably cost Hertz money, but the exposure was incalculable.

Business was good for Shelby, but he was always on the lookout for sales opportunities. He found out that Hertz Rent-A-Car had a Hertz Sports Car Club, a program for high-end travelers with good driving records. Chevrolet Corvettes were available, and Shelby wanted a piece of the action. He approached Peyton Cramer, who in turn met Hertz officials. On November 23, 1965, Hertz Rent-A-Car placed an order for 200 1966 GT350s, followed on December 21, 1966, for 800 more. The Hertz order eventually accounted for about 40 percent of Shelby's 1966 production.

The GT350Hs were mildly modified Shelby production vehicles. Unlike regular GT350s, the Hertz cars came with a back seat and radio. The first 85 units were equipped with four-speeds, and the rest were fitted with automatics. Shelby's auto-box had a different carburetor, and the manual transmission models were equipped with the Autolite 460 model. Most of them came black with gold stripes, but various other colors were used in the production run. This included white, red, blue, and green. All were adorned with the twin racing stripes. Interiors could be any color desired, as long as that desire was for black.

Under the hood lurked your standard Shelby-modified 289-ci screamer. Horsepower was still 306 at 6,000 rpm, and torque remained unchanged at 329 foot-pounds at 4,200 revs. All the standard Shelby mods were left intact, such as functional rear brake cooling ducts and the Monte Carlo bar across the engine compartment. The brakes, complete with competition metallic pads and linings, were also retained from the regular production GT350s. The brakes had to be warmed in order to function properly, and unfortunately many customers found that the cold brakes didn't work. Too often, the H's front-end sheet metal acted as a brake as the car contacted an object. First boosters were installed and then softer brake materials were added. Covering the brakes were chrome-plated steel wheels, 14 -by-6-inch Magnum 500s manufactured by the Motor Wheel Corporation. Ground contact was maintained using 6.95-by-14-Goodyear Blue Streak tires.

Rental cars being rental cars, I suspect that GT350Hs were driven with a touch more enthusiasm than, oh say, a Nova. In 1968 and 1969, Hertz rented current Shelbys again, but without the "H" graphic on the side and with a bit less fanfare. The program worked. Hertz raised its profile in the battle with Avis, and Shelby sold a pack of cars. In these litigious times, it's hard to believe that anyone over 25 with a good record could slap down $17 a day and pay 17 cents a mile to drive a supercar down the road.

## CHAPTER TWO

## THE ARRIVAL OF BIG-BLOCK HIGH PERFORMANCE

Detroit has a habit of bringing out a new vehicle, lithe and trim, then adding mass in the name of public desire. Ford realized that the Mustang needed to grow to meet the increasing competition. General Motors was about to release the new Camaro/Firebird. The Pontiac GTO was building a cult following. Plymouth's Barracuda was improving. Ford realized its rivals were going to be installing big-block engines, and Ford was not going to be left behind in the horsepower wars.

The Mustang was the logical recipient of the FE-series big-block engines in FoMoCo's stable. The problem was the 390-ci engine wouldn't fit between the front suspension of the first-generation Mustang. The new model Mustang rode on the same wheelbase

In the ever-growing horsepower war, Ford responded with the 1967 Mustang GTA, a 325-horsepower 390-ci V-8 mated to an automatic transmission. The tiny A behind the GT label on the rocker panel denoted that this 390-ci Mustang was equipped with an automatic transmission.

Fog lamps mounted in the grille were for GTs only. The extractor scoops on the hood were for show only. Simulated brake cooling vents in front of the rear tires were a feature on the 1967 models.

as the original–108 inches. But every other dimension grew. Overall length increased 2.0 inches to 183.6, while the width increased 2.7 inches to 70.9. Wheel track, the distance between same axle wheels, grew 2.0 inches. This opened up room in the engine compartment.

These changes turned the Mustang from a nimble sports coupe into more of a Grand Touring car. The public loved it. While overall sales fell from 1966 levels, the 472,121 units sold kept the Mustang in the black and filling garages. These were the years when Total Performance ramped up to unbelievable levels.

### THE 1967 MUSTANG GT390

Buyers wanting a fire-breathing Mustang for model year 1967 had more choices. The Hi-Po 271-horsepower 289 V-8 was a strong, flexible power-plant and was still available for $433.55. The relatively lightweight mill helped the vehicle maintain cornering agility. But only 472 such engines were ordered for the car because most buyers were searching for tire-melting performance. So they opted for the "Thunderbird Special," a 390-ci iron block mill that delivered more brutish power for less money. For only $263.71, the customer got 320 ponies and 427 foot-pounds of torque under the long hood. Fitted with this engine and a comfortable amount of optional equipment, the price tag was in the vicinity of $4,100.

The widened track and front suspension modifications made room for the full-sized powerplant. The lower A-arm was lengthened 2.5 inches, while the upper A-arm pivot point was

Mustang styling significantly changed in 1967. The car's new styling queues included a more rakish appearance below the beltline and a revised grille. The 1967 model retained the three vertical taillight design, but the panel between the lights was now concave. High-performance models featured a chrome strip on the edge of the trunk lid. The dual exhaust was not only for show; a 390-ci engine needs to breathe.

lowered. Not only was there room for the engine itself, but the cast-iron exhaust manifolds, as well as the growing slate of power options, required that extra space. Air conditioning, power steering, and power brakes, as well a score of interior options, pushed the Mustang into GT territory. On the test track, the original Pony Car delivered impressive numbers. In the January 1967 issue of *Car Life*, a 390 Mustang, equipped with a 3.25:1 rear axle ratio, recorded a quarter-mile time of 15.5 seconds at 91.4 miles per hour. Eric Dahlquist of *Hot Rod Magazine* took a 390 2+2 to the drag strip and posted a time of 15.31 seconds at 93.45 miles per hour. The single 600-cfm Holley carburetor was bolted to a cast-iron intake manifold, with primary and secondary passages identical at 1.562 inches. At the other end of the power generation cycle were dual exhausts, standard on the GT.

*Car Life* registered a top speed of 113 miles per hour. With 11.38-inch diameter Kelsey-Hayes front brake rotors and 10.00-inch rear drums, it took a while to bring a Mustang GT to a rapid halt. While the front/rear weight balance of 58/42 did not enhance handling, most big-block buyers were scarcely interested in navigating a tight twisty road.

With the increased size came increased weight. With the 390 under the hood, and a normal level of options, the 'Stang tipped the scale at 3,810 pounds. Straight-line stability was improved from the 1966 model and part of the reason was the Firestone Super Sport Wide Oval tires. The F70x14 rubber was praised by testers of the day, some of them preferring the Firestones to the radials then on the market. But the power steering communicated little road feel. With 3.6 turns lock to lock, and a turning diameter of 37.2 feet, the Mustang was not going to be confused with a true sports car, but it was Ford's new weapon in its battle against the new pony car entries. It paved the way, forever increasing cubic inches and wheelbases. And it whet the appetites of young buyers, who were anxious to drive a vehicle unlike anything driven by their parents. Funny thing, kids of all ages loved the power. Still do.

## THE 1967 SHELBY GT500

When Ford increased the dimensions of the Mustang in 1967, Shelby had no choice than to change as well. The first-generation Shelbys were bred to dominate in the SCCA's B-Production class and found that the new market for sport racers favored cubic inches. For 1967, Shelby still offered the GT350, complete with the 306-horsepower, 289-ci small-block. The increased size of the engine compartment allowed Shelby to shoehorn a much larger engine into it–the 428-ci V-8. It was called the GT500, if for no other reason than the number was larger than that of the competition. Some 47 were sold with the famed 427-ci side-oiler engine, but this engine was difficult to drive on the street. This powerplant was in its element at the racetrack. One such engine was installed in the GT500 and was driven by Carroll Shelby for tire testing. This "Super Snake" dynoed at close to 500 horsepower and could reach the upper end of 170 miles per hour.

The 390 GT was Ford's big-block challenger for 1967. Due to the weight of the big-block engine, the car performed admirably in a straight line but was not a serious canyon carver.

But for street driving, the vast majority of the 2,048 GT500s built came with the hydraulic lifter–equipped 428-ci engine, rated at 355 horsepower at 5,400 rpm. Tire-smoking torque was listed at 420 foot-pounds at 3,200 revs, which was enough to quickly waste the Goodyear Speedway 350 E70x15 rubber. The cast-iron block had a 10.5:1 compression ratio and a bore and stroke of 4.13 x 3.98 inches. A "Police Interceptor" cam was installed, and an aluminum medium-rise dual-plane intake manifold, topped with a pair of Holley 650-cfm four-barrel carburetors (Model R-2804 in front and R-2805 in rear) and a progressive

linkage handled fuel induction.

Inside the engine, the crankshaft and pistons were cast items, but the connecting rods were forged. *Car and Driver* magazine flogged one in the February 1967 issue, and the results were indicative of the big-hammer musclecar approach. From 0 to 60 took 6.5 seconds, and the quarter-mile was attacked in 15.0 seconds at 95 miles per hour. Their test vehicle was equipped with the optional $50 C-6 Cruise-O-Matic three-speed automatic transmission and a 3.50:1 rear axle ratio, for a top speed of 128 miles per hour at 5,400 rpm. This showed that the vehicle was

A huge air cleaner covered the large FE-series 390-ci engine. While the optional engine only costs $263.71, its 427 foot-pounds of twist provided scintillating acceleration and could lay waste to a set of tires.

leaning toward boulevard cruising, unlike the GT350's road racing bent. The front/rear weight distribution of 56.4/43.6 percent did little for carving corners, but weight transfer under heavy acceleration was impressive. The large engine added 176 pounds to the front tires, not what a road racing car needed. Speaking of heft, the GT500 tipped the scales at 3,370 pounds, and the $4,195 price tag was within a couple of hundred dollars of a big-block Corvette.

Like the Chevrolet sports car, fiberglass was used in the body, though the Shelby GT500 used fiberglass stylistic and aerodynamic bolt-on pieces, such as the extended nose, air scoops, and spoilers. The first batch of cars put the high beam headlights in the center of the grille, a strong styling statement that ran afoul of the California Department of Motor Vehicles regulation regarding the spacing of the lights. After the first 20 production cars were manufactured, the lamps were moved to the outside edges of the grille, predating the 1969 production Mustang. The relocated

headlights helped increase airflow to the radiator and helped in cooling the sizable engine. The engine also had to supply power to such mandatory options as power brakes and steering, and the popular $356.09 air conditioning option. The pounds were adding up, and the focus was changing. Pure racing was out. Grand Touring was in. The GT500 was just a reflection of the time.

### THE 1968½ 428 COBRA JET

It was no April Fool. Introduced on April 1, 1968, an FE-based big block was slipped between the strengthened front shock towers to help the Mustang compete in the ever hotter muscle arena. The Camaro, Firebird, AMX, GTO, and Barracuda were grabbing headlines and customers from Ford. The pieces for a leading-class vehicle were on the shelf, but until the Cobra Jet was released, the Mustang found itself falling behind the competition. All that changed in April.

In the mid-1960s, the nation's number one Ford dealer was Robert Tasca, in East Providence, Rhode Island. A fan of motorsports, he had sponsored a long list of winning drag-race cars. But he was less than satisfied with the power output from the high-performance production Mustangs. After an employee burned down a 390-engined GT coupe one evening, the dealership cobbled

**Following pages**
With displacement increasing across the gamut of musclecars, it would only be a matter of time before a big-block Shelby was offered. The first 428-ci GT500 was released in 1967. The following year Shelby took the incredibly fast GT500 and made it faster by offering an even more exclusive GT500 KR. The KR moniker stood for "King of the Road," and in actuality few musclecars could challenge it for street supremacy. The standard engine pumped out 335 horsepower while the KR engine produced a whopping 400 horsepower.

together a big-block engine, using a 428 Police Interceptor short block and a pair of 427 low-riser heads. A GTA 390 hydraulic cam and a 735-cfm Holley carburetor were installed as well. The hybrid creation ran the quarter-mile at 13.39 seconds at 105 miles per hour.

This vehicle got good press, and good press was not wasted on Ford. Quickly, the engineering team at Ford built the Cobra Jet engine, using parts on the shelves. They started with a 428 block that was recast in a nodular iron alloy, with more material in the ribbing. For cost considerations, two-bolt main bearings were retained, but this was not going to be a "racing" engine, so two bolts held the meaty connecting rods. The cast-aluminum piston helped get the 10.6:1 compression ratio needed to develop 335 horsepower at 5,600 rpm. The heads were 427 items, the 2.06-inch intake valves and 1.625-inch exhaust valves working to produce 445 foot-pounds at 3,400 revs, enough to merge into most traffic.

Sitting on the aluminum intake manifold was a single 735-cfm Holley four-barrel carburetor. The camshaft was lifted from the 390 GT,

These handsome 10-spoke, 15-inch cast-aluminum wheels are collector's items today. The cobra emblem on the center cap is the same used on today's Cobra model.

The rubber seal on top of the air cleaner mated up to the bottom of the hood, and the scoops fed cool, outside air to the Cobra-Jet 428-ci engine. The huge engine was shoehorned into the engine bay; notice the tight fit between the valve covers and the shock towers.

with lift specs of 0.481/0.490 (intake/exhaust), while duration was 290 degrees.

From the outside, it didn't scream performance. The 428 Cobra Jet option meant that the Mustang was a GT, period. But any of the three body types–coupe, fastback, or convertible–could get the big-block engine. The functional hood scoop was tasteful yet sedate, and the stripe running the length of the hood a nod to performance past. A narrow side stripe looped around the rear quarter scoop, and GT wheels completed the external package. Under the sheet metal, a number of

**Right**
Released in 1967, the 428-ci Cobra Jet was a mixture of off-the-shelf parts that resulted in a strong engine. In standard Ford dress, the 428 Cobra Jet produced 335 horsepower. The 428 in the KR was fitted with larger heads, oversized intake manifold, and a Holley 735 carburetor, and that helped the engine pump out 400 horsepower. *Randy Leffingwell*

The Cobra Jet option was an excellent way to suck in a racer, then promptly blow his doors off. The wheels saw widespread use in 1969 with the next generation of Mustangs. The Cobra Jet was only available in the coupe body style. *Randy Leffingwell*

Chrome valve cleaners and an aluminum intake manifold hint at the tone that the 428-ci Cobra Jet engine took. Under the huge air cleaner was a single 735-cc Holley carburetor. This package generated an impressive 445 footpounds of torque. *Randy Leffingwell*

mandatory options helped maintain control, such as the front power 11.38-inch disc brakes and the aforementioned braced front shock towers. Staggered rear shocks accompanied the four-speed CJ. The right side shock mounted in front of the rear axle in an attempt to reduce axle hop under heavy acceleration. A 31-spline axle was installed to minimize breakage, while the 9-inch rear end

In case the occupants didn't notice the exterior graphics, the script in the center of the dash let everyone know that this was not a grocery-getter Mustang. The T-handle on the shifter was connected to the automatic transmission. *Randy Leffingwell*

could be filled with 3.50:1, 3.91:1, or 4.30:1 gears. It all worked wonderfully together to produce a package that could only come from Detroit.

So what kind of bragging rights did $434 buy? Big ones. The March 1968 issue of *Hot Rod* magazine reported that Eric Dahlquist drove a 3.89:1 limited-slip, rear-axle ratio–equipped one down a drag strip in 13.56 seconds, crossing the finish line at 106.64 miles per hour. This wasn't bad for a four-seater weighing 3,240 pounds. The car bolted from 0 to 60 in 5.9 seconds, which topped the Shelby GT500's time of 6.2 seconds. The Goodyear Polyglas Wide-Oval tires never stood a chance. This was the beginning of sheer brute power, reasonably priced. You had to be a fool to run against one.

## CHAPTER THREE

# ULTIMATE MUSCLE AND THE GENERATION AFTER

The barbarians were at the gate. Hell, they ran it over. The vehicles that were rolling off of the production lines could only be called stupidly fast. Power output was rising faster than a Saturn V rocket, and many street cars exceeded the performance of pure race cars built only a couple of years before. Yet the push was on to raise the bar even higher.

Sales of selected models were directly related to competition, and vice versa. The battle between cross-town rivals Ford and Chevrolet was glowing white-hot, and the public could enjoy the fallout by signing on the dotted line. Even popular slang of the day found its way onto the side of automobiles. The vehicles had what it took under the hood, and they looked the part. There was no

The Boss 302 was built to homologate the racing version, actively raced in the famed SCCA Trans-Am series. It wasn't a mere musclecar; it was a supercar. Fitted with a high-tech 290-horsepower 302 small block and equipped with critical suspension upgrades, the Boss was brutally fast and handled superbly.

The Boss 302 was one of the most visually exciting Mustangs to ever turn a wheel. The adjustable wing on the trunk grabbed attention, and so did the rear widow louvers or sport slats. The slats sat on hinges at their front edge, and could be lifted up to gain access to the rear window for cleaning.

shortage of sizzle. It was applied with a broad brush, the more outrageous looking the better. These were wild times, and the Mustang was front and center in the pursuit of happiness. If you couldn't move faster than the speed of sound, at least you could be the Boss.

By 1971 the writing was on the wall. Pressure from the insurance industry and government-mandated emissions restrictions spelled doom for the musclecar. The fastback sports-roof Mustang was offered until 1973, albeit with serious softened

compression ratios and reduced horsepower output. In an attempt to adjust to the new world order, Ford released the Mustang II in 1974. Starting with a 1971 Pinto chassis, the engineers massaged the platform to deliver what Lee Iacocca wanted in the next generation Mustang–a small, luxurious vehicle that delivered sporting fun at a reasonable price. It was a foot shorter than the original 1965 Mustang, and when ordered with the optional Ghia luxury package it contained more insulating material than the Lincoln Continental.

Former Chevrolet stylist Larry Shinoda was responsible for the Boss's appearance. He designed the Boss 302 graphic package and deleted the nonfunctional rear quarter brake ducts. The same graphics package was used on the Trans Am Boss 302 race cars, which added to the allure of this illustrious car. In 1969 the Boss 302 option set a buyer back $3,788. Today, a low-mileage, unmolested example will typically fetch $20,000 or more.

Sales were soft, to the tune of only 18,000 Mustang IIs hitting the street in the first month. But things changed the next month when OPEC turned off the oil wells. Suddenly the diminutive pony car was "the right car at the right time." By 1978 a low-production, high-performance Mustang was offered. It was called the King Cobra.

## THE 1969 BOSS 302

Whoever said racing improved the breed could use the Boss 302 as its poster car. In 1968, Ford found itself in a position of needing to build the Boss 302. Actually, Ford needed a production car to counter the Chevrolet Camaro Z/28 on the racetrack. The Dearborn firm was up to its axles

in fighting for wins in the SCCA Trans-Am series. Ford had won the prestigious series in 1966 and 1967, but Chevrolet took home the trophy and the bragging rights in 1968. This just wouldn't do at Ford. The Tunnel Port 302 engine had come up short, so engineering set about developing an engine that would level the playing field on the back straight at Riverside Raceway in California. Their efforts coincided with the arrival of a walking dynamo.

Semon "Bunkie" Knudsen been very influential at Chevrolet, a staunch believer of "Winning on Sunday, Selling on Monday." In 1968 he went to Ford and started revving up the company's profile on the track. Bunkie knew of the Z/28 and knew that Ford would get its clock cleaned unless an agile, strong racer in the mold of the mid-1960s Shelby GT350 was developed. SCCA rules required that at least 1,000 of the production version would be built, a challenge that Ford was more than willing to meet.

Knudsen got the ball rolling, but another former Chevrolet employee was instrumental in styling and naming of the new model. Larry Shinoda, designer of the famed 1963 Sting Ray and Mako Shark show cars, made the move to the Blue Oval in mid-May 1968. He, like Bunkie, knew that the youth market was interested in vehicles that could frighten the center stripes off the surface of a curvy road. Shinoda had his finger on the pulse of America's kids, and he forwarded the slang phrase "Boss" to the boardroom for consideration on the sport version of the newly expanded, again, Mustang. The execs gave a collective thumbs down, but Bunkie got it—and he saw that the rest of upper management got it too.

The green light was finally given for Shinoda's design, including the large front and rear spoilers, rear window slats, and bold paint and tape graphics.

By 1969, America had reached the height of the horse-power wars. The 1969 Mach 1 was Ford's chosen weapon. Available with a 351, 390, or 428 V-8, there was a power-plant option to suit every driver. The Mach 1 featured the timeless "SportsRoof" fastback body profile, a classy styling package, and a suspension similar to the Boss 302.

Besides, Bunkie liked to win, both on and off the track. So no small amount of engineering effort was spent to make both the street and track versions of the Boss 302 first in wins and sales. While Kar Kraft built the 450-horsepower racers, the street copy was rolled down the standard assembly line, slowly being fitted with enough mechanical improvements to turn the pony car into arguably the best Mustang built during the musclecar era.

During the 1968 Trans-Am season, Ford ran the Tunnel Port 302, a race-only engine that had a propensity for prematurely expiring. Okay, it would croak before the checkered flag flew. For the 1969 season, things would be different. First, Ford actually built the required 1,000 street-version cars. Second, while the engine still displaced 302 ci, that was about all it shared with its troublesome predecessor.

Ford started with a four-bolt main bearing block, the C8. It was part of the Windsor family of engines. Later in the 1969 production run, C9 or DO castings were used, but the basic configuration remained the same. Bore and stroke was 4.0 by 3.0 inches. Almost all of the entire reciprocating mass was of forged construction. The crankshaft was cross-drilled forged steel, the forged connecting rods used 3/8-inch bolts, and the forged aluminum domed pistons used 5/64-inch compression rings and 3/16-inch oil rings.

The "Boss" heads were lifted from the new 351 Cleveland engine. This was the single largest contributor to the performance that was

To extract maximum power and reliability, Ford put its engineering might behind the Boss 302 engine. The 290-horsepower small block featured large heads with massive valve ports, four-bolt main bearing caps, aluminum windage tray, forged steel connecting rods and crank, forged aluminum pistons, and a massive Holley 780 carburetor. Peak power was made at 5,800-rpm, enough to run the quarter-mile in less than 15 seconds. With the 4.3 Detroit Locker rear end, the Boss galloped from 0 to 60 miles per hour in 5.5 seconds.

unleashed. The heads were found to have the same bolt-hole pattern and bore spacing as the block. T-valve ports within these heads were large enough to swallow common household pets. Canted to produce a polyangular combustion chamber, the 1.71-inch exhaust valve looked puny next to the 2.23-inch intake. The valves were tilted to allow tremendous gas flow at both low and high engine speeds, especially high. The rocker arms sat on screw-in studs, and pushrod guide plates kept the valves pointed in the correct direction during tach testing engine speeds. The mechanical camshaft had a duration of 290 degrees for both intake and exhaust valves and an overlap of 58 degrees. Valve lift was considerable at .477 inch. The intake ports measured 2.4 by 1.7-inches and were attached to an aluminum high-rise intake manifold.

A 780-cfm Holley carburetor resided on top of the special manifold. That was a tip-off that this engine was built for more than hauling groceries. With 1.68-inch diameter primaries and secondaries, this manual choke monster could pass enough fuel to allow the driver to watch the gas gauge move.

Needless to say, with its 10.5:1 compression, it was imperative that the owner use premium fuel. The spec sheet said 290 horsepower at

5,800 rpm and 290 foot-pounds of torque at 4,300 revs. To keep from showering the street with hot, oily engine parts, Ford installed a rev limiter, designed to randomly short out cylinders at 6,150 rpm. Street engines typically didn't need to spin that fast to reach maximum power; however, race engines were a different matter.

Getting the power to the ground was the job of the modified suspension. The front end used high-rate (350-pound) springs and Gabriel shock absorbers. A .72-inch stabilizer bar was installed to minimize body lean under hard cornering. In the rear, the familiar live axle held heavy-duty 31 spline axles. Leaf springs (150-pound) and staggered Gabriel shocks tried to hold axle hop to a minimum when getting heavy into the throttle. But pushing the right pedal was *fun!*

In the September issue of *Car Life*, a Boss 302 was put through its paces. The quarter-mile was run in 14.85 seconds at 96.15 miles per hour. The folks at *Car and Driver* (June 1969) put the whip to the Boss, coming up with a drag strip performance of 14.57 seconds at 97.57 miles per hour. While the numbers tell a tale, it's only part of the story.

This was a Mustang built to turn as well as go fast in a straight line. The desire to best the Bowtie crew resulted in a fine road car. Shod with 15.0 by 7.0-inch Goodyear F60x15 Polyglas rubber on Magnum wheels, and a 55.7/44.3-front/rear-weight balance, the Boss 302 navigated turns with the best of them. Because of the 7.0-inch rims, the fenders had to have modified wheel openings to clear the tires. With the rim width, the front spindles had to be replaced with units

The styling package included twist hood locks and an attractive tape stripe running down both sides. Stock wheels measured 14x6 inches.

The graceful 15-by-7.0-inch Magnum rims required gently flaring the wheel arches to gain sufficient tire clearance. Suspension enhancements included oversized front spindles, shock tower braces, large front sway bar, staggered high-performance shocks, front disc brakes, and 16:1 steering ratio.

having larger wheel bearings. Told you Ford was serious about getting the Boss to run.

If you wanted an automatic transmission, well, too bad. A wide-ratio four-speed top-loader manual box, with a 2.78 first gear handled gear changes, while a 3.50:1 rear axle ratio was on the other end of the driveshaft. A close-ratio gearbox with a 2.32 first gear was available, however.

This much excitement didn't come cheap: A normally equipped Boss 302 went for about $3,788, while the standard Mustang SportsRoof went for about $2,618. Money well spent? Oh yes. Ford built 1,628 Boss 302s in 1969, and news of the vehicle got out to the tune of 7,013 in 1970, the last year of Boss 302 production. Was it worth

Equipped with air conditioning, power steering, and other comfort features, the 335 horsepower 428-ci engine still had enough power to turn quarter-mile times in the high 14-second range. The Shaker hood was a popular option, allowing the world to watch as the engine shook as the accelerator was depressed.

it to Ford? Oh yes. While the Camaro won the Trans-Am title in 1969, the Blue Oval was finally victorious in 1970, the Boss 302 bringing home the trophy.

Bunkie was a happy man, and the Mustang mystique was burnished just a little bit brighter.

### THE 1969 MACH 1 428 COBRA JET

Image is powerful. The Mustang was definitely about image. Ever since Job 1 rolled down the assembly line, the original pony car projected an aura of youth and excitement. Buyers wanting a healthy dose of verve could order any number of sporty versions, culminating in mid-1968 in the Cobra Jet–equipped GT. But the styling was starting to look a bit dated. The Mustang's competitors were rolling out fresh sheet metal, and the resulting sales put pressure on Ford to restore the 'Stang to the head of the pack. So in the finest Detroit fashion, the Mustang grew again. While the wheelbase stayed the same at 108 inches, overall vehicle length grew 3.8 inches, all of it in the front.

When the Mach 1 option debuted in 1969, it was a well-balanced, sporting Grand Touring vehicle. Available only with the SportsRoof (fastback) model, the replacement for the GT came with plenty of flash, and when properly optioned, plenty of fast. As a kind of high-powered boulevard cruiser, Ford fitted the Mach 1 with 55 pounds of insulation. While the Mach 1 was Ford's top high-performance SportsRoof Mustang, it could be fitted with the machinery needed to put a smile on a tire salesman's face. That machinery was called the 428 Cobra Jet.

The styling of the 1969 Mach 1 garnered compliments from all quarters. The aggressive front end was fitted with four headlights, the only year that Mustangs would be so equipped. Vehicles

The tilt steering wheel swings away to allow easy entry. Squeezing the gasket that ran the circumference of the steering activated the horn. Genuine wood-grain appliqué added warmth to the interior, while the Comfortweave upholstery covered the seats, and a large clock faced the front seat passenger.

destined to break the speed of sound came with hood pins as standard, but they could be left off. The vents that had been found on the side of the car in front of the rear wheels were now moved to the area just below the rear quarter windows. Still, they stressed form over function.

At the rear, the concave panel was still flanked by three vertical tail lamp lenses, and the small tail spoiler gave the Mach 1 a Trans-Am look, if not quite the performance. The lower body stripe was made of reflective tape that glowed at night when headlights struck it. The interior was decked out

with high-back seats covered in "Comfortweave", genuine simulated teak wood appliqué by the acre, and basic instrumentation. A console ran down the center of the interior, and a large clock faced the passenger, no doubt ready for the next rally. Depressing a rubber strip that ran the circumference of the steering wheel activated the Rim-Blow steering wheel's horn. The view over the hood was spectacular, the sound track thrilling, and the thrust was ready and on cue.

Under the long hood was one of three engines. The standard Mach 1 mill was the 351-ci

Simulated rear brake–cooling ducts were fitted to the area below the rear side windows. The flat black finish on the hood reduced reflections, and the hood pins were a nice high-performance touch.

Windsor, topped with a two-barrel carburetor and making all of 250 horsepower. Next up the 351-ci ladder was the four-barrel carbureted version helping to generate 290 horsepower. But for those who wanted something with presence, the 428 Cobra Jet was top dog. This was essentially the same engine offered in the 1968 Mustang, same 10.6:1 compression, same huge single four-barrel carb, same 335 rated horsepower. This engine could be installed in any of the three body models of Mustang, but when installed in the Mach 1, well, it was a match made in *gearhead* heaven.

The 428 Cobra Jet was basically a drag racing engine in search of a fight. With the 428 big-block holding the front tires down, the front/rear weight distribution of 59.3/40.7

meant that the Boss 302 driver would not need to worry on a twisty road. But the Mach 1 was about styling, about exuding a menacing presence. With the stock 14-inch Goodyear Polyglas tires on 6-inch rims, the brutal torque, 440 foot-pounds (3,400 rpm) worth, could–and would–overpower the rubber contact patches.

Ordering the Cobra Jet option put the "Competition Handling" suspension under the 3,607-pound musclecar. This included higher rate front and rear springs, a stiff antisway bar, and staggered rear shocks when the four-speed manual transmission was installed. The power brakes featured single-piston caliper front discs, and rear drums were an option that made sense with that much iron in the lead. Even so, brake

In order to fit the massive Boss 429 into the engine bay, a number of suspension modifications had to be carried out. The shock towers were revamped and the suspension mounting points were relocated. The 429 rode on Magnum 500 15-by-7-inch wheels, and like the Boss 302, the front spindles were massaged for strength and wheel-well clearance.

performance was less than stellar, *Car and Driver* halting a 428 Mach 1 in 256 feet from 80 miles per hour.

But the Mach 1 was not built to stop. It was made to rear its nose in the air and howl down a stretch of pavement. In a January 1969 test by the *Popular Hot Rodding* crew, a Cobra Jet Mach 1 flew down the quarter-mile in 13.69 seconds at 103.44 miles per hour with an automatic transmission. The scribes at *Car and Driver* didn't make it to the finish line at such a pace; 14.3 seconds showed on the clock, while the speedometer read 100 miles per hour over the finish line. Their vehicle, using an automatic and 3.91:1 gears in the rear axle, generated a top speed of 115 miles per hour. The midrange torque was quite impressive, with a firm push from 40 to 80

miles per hour. Under heavy acceleration, the suspension predictably squatted and the driver's compartment was filled with the sound of a throaty, howling big-block V-8. It was an image that Detroit fostered, and the reality was even better than the dream.

## THE 1969 BOSS 429

If the Boss 302 was a rapier, the Boss 429 was a broadsword. A tool built to cut a wide swath in NASCAR competition, but it also successfully competed in NHRA and AHRA stock classes. This monster never would have seen the street if it had not been for the racing regulations that called for the engine to be available to the public. Yet Ford was deep into competing with the rest of Detroit on Sunday. The Chrysler Hemi and Chevrolet's Rat engines were kicking ass and taking names, and Ford wasn't going to be left as the perennial runner-up.

Ford needed a new race engine for the Torino Talladega and Mercury Cyclone. Marketing was convinced that it would be a lot easier selling a high-powered Mustang to the public than a big-block intermediate. An agreement was reached with NASCAR officials in which Ford had to install at least 500 new engines in the Boss 429 in

**Following pages**

The Boss 429 is one of the best and certainly one of the most exclusive big-block Mustangs ever built. The Boss 429 was essentially a racing engine crammed into the tight confines of the 1969–1970 Mustang SportsRoof. Like the Boss 302, the Boss 429 was created, so Ford would comply with minimum build rules of NASCAR stock car racing. Although the 429 was a competent musclecar, it didn't realize its potential in stock form due to a mild cam and a small carburetor. When a Boss 429 engine was given an aggressive cam, a larger carburetor, and large headers, it could battle Hemis.

order for the engine to be in race versions of the Cyclones and Talledegas.

Enter the "385" family of engines. Introduced in 1968, this thin-wall design engine, in 429- and 460-ci incarnations, saw duty in the Thunderbird and Lincolns. The Ford engineers didn't cook up a low-revving luxury cruiser engine, however. This was a racing engine. Basic block architecture was passenger-car 429, but it was cast from nodular iron. The heads differed in almost every possible respect from the standard 429.

They were made from aluminum, in an attempt to hold weight down. The 429-ci engine with prototype iron heads weighed in at more than 900 pounds. The alloy heads used a valve-train arrangement that saw the valve stems going in apparently random directions. In fact, the combustion chambers were semi hemispherical. The

nickname "twisted Hemi" came from the valve angle, and "Blue Crescent" was derived from the Blue Oval and the shape of the chambers. The heads were sealed to the iron block using copper rings and O-rings instead of head gaskets. Inside the heads were massive valves, meant to put large

The massive Boss 429 was derived from the 385 series engines. Its features included O-rings instead of head gaskets to seal the heads to the block, semi-hemispherical combustion chambers, massive cylinder heads and mammoth ports, and four-bolt main bearing caps. Due to the tight fit in the engine compartment, power accessories were not installed, and the battery was installed in the trunk.

The Boss 429 carried a simple straightforward styling package. A small outlined graphic on the front fender denoted that this was a Boss 429. Differing from the Boss 302, the 1969 429 carried fake brake duct scoops and C-pillar badges, but the rear deck spoiler was an option. The Boss 429 conversion was done at Kar Kraft, Ford's semi-official race shop. The engine was designed to compete on the tracks of NASCAR.

The huge hood scoop was functional and distinctive. Any engine as large as the Boss 429's needed a massive amount of fresh air. Its aggressive design complemented the fastback lines of the body.

amounts of racing fuel into contact with the forged aluminum pistons. The intake valves were 2.29 inches in diameter, and the valve seat cut at 30 degrees. The exhausts measured in at 1.91 inches, and the seats cut at 45 degrees. Valve lift was .440–inch, and duration was 296 degrees exhaust, 282 degrees intake, and was activated by a hydraulic camshaft.

The bore and stroke was 4.36 by 3.59 inches. Holley's 735-cfm four-barrel, model C9AF-9510-S, sat atop an aluminum intake manifold. The 10.5:1 compression helped to deliver a rated 375 horsepower at 5,200 rpm, and the torque rating of 410 foot-pounds arrived at 3,400 revs. The cross-drilled, forged crankshaft was attached to forged connecting rods. In fact, there were two versions of the Boss 429 engine, the S and T editions. The S engine sported NASCAR-grade connecting rods that used huge rod bolts that weighed almost 3 pounds each. The T engine had standard production con rods.

With such a huge engine, the Mustang was woefully short of room under the hood. Considerable modifications were needed to squeeze the detuned race motor into the pony car. There was no way that Ford could assemble the minimum 500 vehicle on the regular line, so the job was farmed out to Kar Kraft, Ford's quasi-official race shop in Brighton, Michigan. Ford would ship Mustang SportsRoof bodies that were meant to hold 428 SCJ engines. Kar Kraft widened the engine bay by moving the front shock towers outward, and relocated the suspension mounting points down and outward 1 inch. An export brace helped tie the cowl to the shock towers to retain strength. Due to the tight confines under the hood with the enormous engine, the 85-amp battery was moved to the relatively spacious trunk. Air conditioning was not available because there was no room for the bulky components.

External modifications were rather low-key, a deep front spoiler and front fender decals. An enormous functional hood scoop sat on top of the hood, looking like it would be at home at Daytona. Chrome "Magnum 500" steel wheels were surrounded by Goodyear Polyglas F60x15 tires. The 7-inch rim width required fender modifications for tire clearance. Under the skin, the front spindles were beefed up, just like the Boss 302. The brakes were identical to those on the Boss 302, with power front disc and rear drums. Shock absorbers were heavy-duty Gabriel units, and the live rear axle contained standard 3.91:1 gears in a Traction-Lok differential.

Gear sets from 3.50:1 to a Detroit Locker 4.30:1 were available, depending on the desired acceleration rate. Because of the added weight

On the interior side, the Boss 429 was nearly identical to its standard SportsRoof and less powerful brethren. The instruments were buried in deep tunnels in the dash and were easy to read.

The concave panel between the triple vertical taillights continued in the 1969 model year. The original dealer sticker used the Shelby Cobra design as its highly recognizable emblem.

over the front tires, a rear 0.62-inch antisway was installed to counter the effects of understeer. A 0.94-inch front bar worked to minimize body roll. After all, the big Boss 429 did have a front/rear weight distribution of 56/44.

And how did the Boss 429 perform on the street? Like an emasculated race car engine, which in street trim is essentially what it was. With the relatively small carburetor, mild camshaft, and rev limiter, the Boss 429 didn't conquer the competition like a Hemi-powered Mopar. It produced a less-than-spectacular 0 to 60 time of 7.1 seconds, while the drag strip was tackled in 14.9 seconds, with a trap speed of 102.85 miles per hour. The velocity at the finish line indicated that the Boss 429 was coming into the heart of its powerband at the end of the strip. Like most Hemi design engines, mid- and upper-range power was their forte. The Boss 429 was no different.

A 428 CJ Mach 1 would hold its own in most street contests with the Boss 429. If a larger carburetor, headers, and a more aggressive camshaft were fitted, however, the engine came alive, generating sinful amounts of power– power that was on par with Hemis and LS-6-powered cars. Then the broadsword would swoop down, smiting the infidels. In an age of large, the Boss 429 was a legend in its own time, and now.

## THE 1971 BOSS 351

The original pony car had grown to Clydesdale proportions. Ford was on a two-year styling cycle, and the Mustang was no exception. Growth in all directions was the norm. Detroit was living by the bigger-is-better creed. The wheelbase was stretched to 109 inches; the overall length increased 2.1 inches to 189.5 inches. Width was up 2.4 inches, and the average vehicle weight was 500 pounds more than that of the 1970 models. The Mustang was bulking up.

One of the reasons for the increased heft was the need to fit monster-sized powerplants between the front shock towers without heavily modifying the engine compartment. The 429-ci Cobra Jet was still on the option sheet for the last time, and the Boss 302 was absent in 1971. But the spirit of that capable road missile lived on for one more year in the Boss 351. Ford had stepped away from racing, which was the reason the Boss line of Mustangs was created in the first place. Ford announced its departure from competition two days before the Boss 351 debuted at the Detroit Auto Show.

From a dynamic standpoint, it was one of the most capable 'Stangs Ford had built to date. But the

insurance companies had started to put serious pressure on the auto industry to build more socially responsible (milder) vehicles. In addition, the government-mandated emission standards were sucking the performance out of automobiles like a swarm of leeches. So inevitably the musclecar craze faded.

But the Mustang stepped away from the pulpit of speed in fine fashion. The formula of a high-revving, high-output small-block engine installed in a responsive chassis worked in the late 1960s, and it worked in 1971. A 351 Cleveland engine was the starting point, and the four-bolt main bearing caps provided stability on the bottom end. The bore and stroke of 4.0 by 3.5 inches gave the 351 engine the same bore as the Boss 302 and a 1/2-inch longer stroke. Extruded pop-up aluminum pistons were attached to magnafluxed forged connecting rods that attached to a Brinell-tested cast crankshaft. A pair of Boss 302 heads, featuring modified cooling passages, complete with 2.195-inch intake valves and 1.714-inch exhaust valves, sat on top of the cast-iron block. The poly-angle heads were built to flow well at high rpms. To this end, the mechanical camshaft was more radical than the previous Boss small block. Valve lift was a healthy .491 inch, while the duration of both intake and exhaust valves was 324 degrees.

Metering the fuel/air mixture was the responsibility of the 750-cfm Autolite Spread Bore four-barrel carburetor. The primaries were only 1.56 inches in diameter, the better to stretch mileage. But the 1.96-inch secondaries looked like a couple of manholes on top of the engine. An aggressive 11.0:1 compression allowed the engine to produce 330 horsepower at 5,400 rpm. The max torque of 370 foot-pounds was delivered at 4,000 rpm. An electronic rev limiter cut out spark to cylinders at 6,150 rpm. And the only

This was the last year that the hood carried functional air scoops. Twist locks, giving a cleaner appearance, replaced pin hood locks. The argent-colored chin spoiler was susceptible to scrapes.

**Left**

The Boss 302 and 429 were discontinued after 1970. With Ford no longer officially involved in racing, a high-performance 351 was given the Boss name. Although the Boss 351 was the last of the Boss line, it had superb handling and was an extremely fast musclecar. The small-block screamer could reach 60 miles per hour from a stop in less than 6 seconds, and it could cover the quarter-mile in the low 14s.

transmission installed was the top-loader four-speed manual, complete with Hurst shifter.

The functional Ram-Air NACA ducts on the hood fed cool, dense air to the engine at speed. In the February 1971 issue of *Car and Driver*, the Boss 351 posted 14.1 seconds at 100.6 miles per hour. The all-important 0 to 60 miles per hour in 5.8 was nothing to sneeze at, even at the peak of the musclecar era. In the March 1971 issue of *Road Test*, the Boss 351 took 5.9 seconds to reach 60 miles per hour, on its way to covering the quarter-mile in 13.98 seconds, tripping the finish line lights at 104.1 miles per hour. Top speed was in the vicinity of 117 miles per hour, as off-the-line pull was favored over top speed. The Boss 351 had nothing to apologize for on the track.

Like the Boss 302s that predated the 351, handling was not ignored. Also like the Boss 302s, the Competition Suspension was underneath, with high-rate front coil springs and 53-inch rear leafs. Staggered rear shocks were installed, as well as 11.3-inch front disc brake rotors and 10 by 2-inch rear drums. A front 7/8-inch and a rear 5/8-inch antisway bar helped reduce understeer.

Variable-ratio power steering was installed in a Mustang for the first time. *Car and Driver* had nothing but praise for it, saying, "Easily the most significant of the Mustang's mechanical advancements has been made in the steering. It's not particularly quick on center but it is remarkably precise—certainly as good as the best from Detroit—and small steering corrections can be easily and accurately made."

The dramatic styling was successful in turning heads. The long hood and short rear deck formula was in full flower. From behind the wheel, the hood looked like the flight deck of an aircraft carrier, while the rear window was only

Tape graphics were a popular and inexpensive way for a manufacturer to make a model stand out from the crowd during the musclecar era. The Boss 351 was a prime example, but unlike a couple of years later, the 1971 Boss 351 had the power to back the image.

14 degrees from horizontal. Bold side stripes and hood treatments left no doubt as to the purpose of the Boss 351, the massive front spoiler trying to hold the bow down at high speed. This Boss rode on F60x15 tires on Magnum 500 wheels. The front pair held up 58 percent of the vehicle's weight. Total poundage was 3,860, up more than 300 pounds over the Boss 302. The larger engine helped overcome the heft.

The price of the Boss 351 was hefty as well, with dealers asking $4,124 for the car before options were ladled on. This might be one of the reasons only 1,806 were sold, and another might be the rise in gasoline prices in 1971. For a vehicle that could only get 14 miles per gallon on a good day, cubic inches translated into cubic dollars at the gas station. The introduction of unleaded gasoline in 1972 did nothing for the future of performance. Thus, the Boss line of Mustangs was shown off of the stage. But the Boss 351 was the culmination of a line of streetable race cars that brought glory to Ford. And more than a few thrills to the lucky drivers.

## THE 1978 MUSTANG II KING COBRA

The Gas Crisis had arrived in 1974. Long lines for fuel were making the evening news, and motorists were asked to get America out of the energy crunch by conservation, carpooling, and

The Boss 351 engine was based on 351 Cleveland block that carried a cast-iron timing change cover. Other high-performance features included four-bolt main bearing caps, shot-peened connecting rods, forged pistons, and a solid lifter camshaft.

Like its predecessor, the Boss a 351 was only available with a four-speed manual transmission. The stout Hurst shifter controlled the four-speed gearbox, making the rapid shifting a joy.

common sense. High-powered, loud, fast vehicles were suddenly seen as antisocial as well as very expensive to run. Meanwhile, the legislators in Washington, D.C., were pushing through laws that would significantly reduce emissions from automobiles. This was not a bad idea, except that the technology of the day was not quite up to the task of meeting mandated emission standards and providing good fuel economy and respectable levels of performance. Something had to give.

It was the power part of the equation that got the axe. Small was suddenly desirable. So

Based on the Pinto platform, the reduced size of the Mustang II is evident in a side view. The short wheelbase and long overhang did little toward a smooth ride, contrary to Lee Iacocca's desire for a "little limousine."

Although the 1978 Mustang II King Cobra was a high-performance styling package rather than a bona fide musclecar, it indicated a renewed interest by Ford in high performance. Even though legislation in the early 1970s essentially killed the powerhouse carbureted V-8s, the technology to make real high performance possible was being developed. The King Cobra packed a 302-ci engine that produced a paltry 134 net horsepower, but it showed times were a-changing.

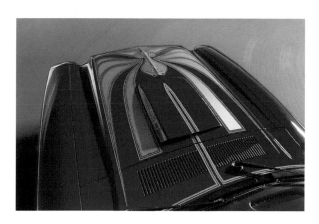

The three-door fastback had almost every gee-whiz styling touch imaginable, including a giant Cobra hood decal, fake hood scoop, and tape stripes, which were strategically placed on the rocker panels, rear deck, and roof.

the timing could not have been better as Ford introduced the next generation Mustang in 1974, a subcompact, small-engined vehicle in the same vein as the original only a decade before. The base engine was a little 140-ci four-cylinder, putting out a pathetic 88 horsepower. Only one motor was offered on the option sheet–a German-built, 105-horsepower, 171-ci V-6.

Riding on a 96.2-inch wheelbase, the little pony car did have a plush ride compared to earlier Mustangs, but with such a short wheelbase interior room suffered. The Mustang II approached 3,000 pounds, and the miniature motors produced miniature performance. Yet the latest incarnation of the original pony car racked up sales approaching 386,000, and *Motor Trend* named it Car of the Year. Yet the desire for a true high-performance Mustang had not diminished. So with the equity of a valued name in the bank, Ford answered the power-starved enthusiasts with the revival of a

performance name–sans performance. With technology lagging behind legislation, and to stave off the disgruntled, Ford had to introduce something, anything. Enter the King Cobra in 1978. At least it reminded us that the Mustang had a high-performance past and it would have a high-performance future. The muscle-car territory now belonged to the Camaro and its corporate cousin, the Firebird. The Mustang now competed with the Chevrolet Monza. Heart be still.

With the introduction of the Mustang II in 1974, the engineers in Dearborn planned to return a V-8 under the hood. This happened in 1975, as a 302-ci engine was stuffed under the hood. It produced only 140 horsepower and was fitted only with an automatic transmission. However, it was a welcome increase over the paltry pony-grade power of 1974. This was the top motor throughout the Mustang II's brief lifetime. While the Mach 1 name was available on the Mustang II, it was little more than a tarted-up fastback model.

In 1976, Ford introduced the Cobra II model, a further ladling on of cosmetic performance. Designed by the father of the Pontiac GTO, Jim Wangers, the Cobra II used large decals, a front air dam, rear spoiler, and heavy black-out treatment to convey the aura of the Cobra mystique of the mid-1960s. Motortown Corporation of Dearborn, Michigan, owned by Wangers, assembled the package. While it couldn't hold a candle to the original snake, it was a good effort from Ford to build a vehicle aimed at the enthusiasts.

In the best tradition of Detroit, nothing succeeds like excess. At this point in the Mustang's history, it was external gewgaws that were rolling the vehicles off showrooms. So Gene

The plush interior was an inviting place to ride. The driver faced a brushed-aluminum instrument panel, tachometer, speedometer, and other essential gauges as well as a factory eight-track tape player. T-tops allowed the sun to shine in while maintaining the structural stiffness needed for good handling.

Boridinat, head of Ford Styling, had his team design a Mustang II that would bring tears of joy to the owners of decal factories. A huge snake was emblazoned on the hood, while a rear-facing, nonfunctional scoop was garnished with a 5.0 sticker denoting the engine size. The $1,253 option was the priciest since the Boss 429. For all that green, a buyer got a fastback Mustang with a large chin spoiler, cross-lace aluminum wheels, and a 302-ci V-8. This version of the evergreen small block generated 134 horsepower at 3,600 rpm, while the 247 foot-pounds of torque came on at 1,800 revs. The 8.4:1 compression could live comfortably with the lower octane unleaded fuel, while the Motorcraft two-barrel carburetor drew its petroleum from a 16.5-gallon fuel tank.

At least the four-speed manual transmission kept the driver awake during quarter-mile runs. *Car Craft* extracted 17.06 seconds at 80.69 miles per hour at the strip. The scribes at *Cars* tested a King Cobra in their August 1978 issue and came up with a drag strip performance of 16.59 seconds at 82.41 miles per hour, along with 13.4 miles per gallon. It came with a 2.64:1 rear axle ratio, which did nothing for acceleration, but in those times it was necessary to meet the Corporate Average Fuel Economy (CAFÉ) standards.

Under the skin, the King Cobra came with front and rear antisway bars, heavy-duty springs, and adjustable shock absorbers. The front suspension was independent, with unequal-length control arms and coil springs. At the other end, the live rear axle was connected to semi-elliptic leaf springs, just like Mustangs of yore. It also featured power rack and pinion, variable-ratio steering, power front disc brakes, and white letter 195/70R13 wide-oval, steel-belted radial tires. T-tops were available and did little to stiffen the body. But they let the sunlight and wind flood in and increased the fun quotient.

The King Cobra tipped the scales at almost 3,300 pounds. Fully loaded, it cost an incredible $6,890. Getting up to 60 miles per hour could tax drivers' patience, with 11.2 seconds crawling across the face of their Timex. But compared to its peers, the King Cobra was posting respectable numbers.

The King Cobra did not sell in large numbers, with only 4,318 rumbling down the road. The "Boss of the Mustang stable" (Fordspeak) was a respectable attempt to keep the performance flame lit in some very dark years for

The once mighty 302-ci engine had been reduced to 134-net horsepower by 1978. It generated an unspectacular 17.06 quarter-mile run. Heart be still. But at least the V-8 was still alive and available.

Mustang enthusiasts. And the third-generation Mustang was on the horizon. The Mustang IIs, including the King Cobra variant, have been ridiculed and panned by both press and public. But the little 'Stang kept the nameplate alive long enough for technology to progress enough to keep the government, the environmentalists, and motorheads happy. This is more than enough reason to call the King Cobra a Mustang Milestone.

## CHAPTER FOUR

OFFICIAL PAC

63rd. ANNUAL INDIANAPOLIS 500 MILE R

# THE FOX AND
# THE MUSTANG

The Mustang and motorsport have been intertwined since the first model rolled off the assembly line. The engineers in Dearborn worked hard to correct shortcomings of the Pinto-based Mustang II. The result was a vehicle the public loved, and better yet, bought. However, there was only one real high-performance offering during the mid-1970s, the King Cobra, and that had paled in comparison to the Mustangs of yesteryear and the current competition. The five-year-old Mustang II was long in tooth, and the previous year General Motors had re-released the Camaro Z28 to strong reviews.

And one must not forget, the Pontiac Trans Am had gained a loyal following. Many considered it the only bona fide musclecar of

In 1979, Ford unveiled the new Fox-chassis Mustang and ushered in a era of Mustang high performance. The completely redesigned third-generation ponycar featured fine handling and refined styling. It returned to the Brickyard to pace the Indy 500, and Ford released an Indy Pace Car edition Mustang in honor of the new cart. The car carried special paint, trim, and used either a 132-horsepower turbo four or a 140 5.0-liter V-8. The actual Pace Cars used a Roush-built 250-horsepower 5.0-liter V-8. *Randy Leffingwell*

The Pace Car used metric-sized wheels and tires. All 11,000 buyers had a view of the sky with the standard sunroof. It was only available in hatchback form. *Randy Leffingwell*

the mid-1970s. Ford needed a new Mustang challenger for the returning high-performance market.

The third-generation pony car started as a Fox, not the four-legged variety. The platform was derived from the Ford Fairmont/Mercury Zephyr. Under the supervision of Hal Sperlich, the Fox program was started in 1973. He had been instrumental in the creation of the original Mustang, and he wanted a vehicle that could be sold in the United States and Europe. Today, the notion of making several "different" automobiles from a common platform is commonplace. In the mid-1970s, the concept was revolutionary. The North American and European factories used different manufacturing methods, however. In the end, the new Fox would be only a U. S. product. When Ford's North American Automotive Operations

(NAAO) took the development reins in 1975, the die was cast to create a unibody basis for a sporty car as well as a sedan.

The new car closely echoed the first Mustang's dimensions. The wheelbase was lengthened to 100.4-inches, increasing the interior space as well as making the car more stable at speed. Stylist Jack Telnack, fresh from a stint as design vice president at Ford of Europe, and fellow designer Fritz Mayhew created the new lines of the car, which was available as a two-door sedan or a hatchback. Actually, the latter was more a "semi-fastback," the large hatch stamping having a high rear deck that visually separated the rear window from the trunk area as well as improving the vehicle's aerodynamics. The coefficient of drag was 0.44, the lowest the

In the finest Euro tradition, the dial gauges were easy to read. Unfortunately, it still carried an 85-mile-per-hour speedometer. The Recaro-style seats were comfortable and firmly held the driver in place behind the three-spoked wheel during spirited driving. *Randy Leffingwell*

Mustang had ever been. Better yet, weight was down 200 pounds.

## THE 1979 INDY PACE CAR

With the newly styled Mustang on the menu, Ford supplied the Indy 500 Pace Car for 1979, complete with a Jack Roush–built 302-ci engine cranking out 250 horsepower. This mill was tricked out using a Boss 302 forged crank and connecting rods, 351 Windsor heads fitted with large intake and exhaust valves, four-barrel carburetion–the works. Midway through the model year, Ford introduced the street version of this car, complete with special beige metallic paint and striping. Unlike the actual pace car, the production cars were equipped with one of two engines, a turbocharger four cylinder or the trusty 302-ci V-8. The turbo version was a lightweight package that developed 132 horsepower at 4,800 rpm with 6 pounds of boost. The 140-ci iron-block/head SOHC engine was assembled in

The faithful 5.0-liter, 302-ci engine produced a measly 140 horsepower, but it was the closest thing to performance that a Mustang driver could get in 1979. *Randy Leffingwell*

Lima, Ohio, and used a 9.0:1 compression ratio to try to maintain what little low-end torque was available. While the standard nonturbo four-cylinder engine only made 88-horsepower from its two-barrel Motorcraft carburetor, the Garrett AiResearch TO-3 turbo sat under a two-barrel Holley 6500 carburetor. This made for a sprightly powerplant once the turbo spun up and the boost came on. Because of the demands made upon it, the turbo four-banger was fitted with forged pistons and special piston rings. The lubrication system was upgraded, and the valves were sodium-filled for better heat control. These measures helped produce an engine that was an improvement from the stock four-cylinder, but

73

The sticker on the rear quarter left little doubt as to where the source of inspiration came from for the vivid Pace Car edition. The cast-aluminum metric wheels would only accept metric tires, not the sort of rolling stock found in most corner garages. *Randy Leffingwell*

The 1984 Mustang SVO was named after the group that created it—Special Vehicle Operations. The group, headed by Michael Kranefuss, created one of the finest handling and well-mannered Mustangs ever. The fascinating styling features included a smooth front end with improved aerodynamics, important in any vehicle capable of running 140 miles per hour.

Another feature exclusive to the SVO was the bi-level rear wing assembly, which was effective in generating negative lift. The top wing was designed to spill the airflow rearward, so that the air would tumble onto the rear lip of the lower wing, pushing the vehicle down and improving gas mileage.

suffered from durability problems. Turbocharging a street car was in its infancy in the United States, so lessons needed to be learned.

The other engine was the 5.0-liter, 302-ci iron block/heads V-8 that had been under Mustang hoods for years. Ford decided to drop the cubic inch designation and go with the 5.0-liter V-8 moniker. With a compression ratio of 8.4:1, the hydraulic valve lifter engine made 140 horsepower at 3,600 rpm and 250 foot-pounds of twist at 1,800 revs. A two-barrel Motorcraft carburetor sat atop a cast-iron intake manifold, and exhaust gases departed through a single chrome-tipped pipe. Performance figures for the V-8 were good. The new 5.0 scampered from 0 to 60 in 8.3 seconds, the quarter-mile covered in 17.0 seconds at 84.8 miles per hour. The turbo four took 9.1 seconds to get to 60, the drag strip flashing by in 17.4 seconds, while the finish line lights recorded 82.0 miles per hour.

It was easy to tell a Pace Car replica coming down the road. A front air dam, fitted with fog lamps, and a rear-facing, nonfunctional hood scoop were quick clues. The two-tone paint and stripes were available only on the Pace Car, and the decals flanking the sides were put on either at the dealership or in the buyer's driveway. While the actual Pace Cars had a T-top installed, this was still in the prototype stage at Ford, and the 11,000 Pace Car replicas sold had a flip-up moon roof.

The Fox platform was home to a different suspension approach than prior Mustangs. Now the front tires were controlled by a modified MacPherson strut arrangement. The coil spring did not wrap around the strut like most applications, but instead was installed between the lower control arm and the vehicle body. The rear suspension was a departure as well. While not the independent rear setup that many wanted, leaf springs were no longer aboard. A four-bar link and coil springs were attached to the solid rear axle. An antisway bar was fitted at both ends.

Also new was the wheel/tire package. Jack Telnack's time in Europe had shown him that the American way was not the only way. To improve the Mustang's handling, the Pace Car was fitted with Michelin's TRX radials. These tires had a 390-millimeter diameter, so metric-sized forged aluminum wheels were used. The 15.35-inch diameter, 5.9-inch wide rim was a first on an American car and did a lot to turn the Mustang into an exciting drive. The result was a vehicle that could hold its own in a corner with the likes of the Chevrolet Corvette, Porsche 924, and Datsun 280Z.

Slipping behind the wheel into the multi-adjustable Recaro sport seats did wonders in setting an aggressive tone for the Mustang Pace Car.

The intercooled and turbocharged 2.3-liter four produced 175 horsepower at 4,500 rpms and 210 foot-pounds of torque at 3,000 rpms. The seal around the top of the intercooler fitted flush with the bottom of the hood, where a scoop directed cool air across the heat exchanger to cool the air up to 125 degrees.

These seats held the driver and front passenger in during aggressive cornering. Full instrumentation faced the wheelman. Rear tires hopped, spun, and fought for traction under heavy acceleration, especially with the 5.0 liter. Under the right hand was a four-speed transmission; this was mandatory in a musclecar. World Driving Champion Jackie Stewart drove one on the track at Indy, saying, "It seemed very stable. It's more of a high-performance vehicle than the Porsche 924. And I think it is also a darn good-looking motor car."

The Fox platform was the beginning of a Mustang renaissance. Ford had the size right back in 1964, and although the dimensions varied over time, the Mustang returned to the winning formula in 1979. The public responded with enthusiasm,

snapping up 369,936 'Stangs that year. The pony car had survived some scary years, when a fun Mustang meant an older, used model. Ford didn't give up returning the Mustang to the performance path, and it hasn't looked back. The Indy Pace Car signaled that the real race was resuming.

## THE 1984 MUSTANG SVO

The mid-1980s were a time of resurgence. The Soviet Union, only a few years from its demise, boycotted the Los Angeles Olympic games. President Ronald Reagan handily won reelection. And Ford introduced a Mustang that harkened back to the halcyon days of the late 1960s and early 1970s. Fuel prices had stabilized, and technology had progressed to the point that electronics were making what had been impossible only a handful of years before commonplace.

This large NACA duct was fitted into the hood, slightly offset toward the passenger side. It led outside air through the intercooler, boosting power and keeping the fuel economy of a regular four-cylinder. The SVO's 2.3-liter was a better all-around package because it used the Garret AiResearch turbocharger, intercooler, and a new head.

Ford had been involved with motorsports since Henry Ford and Barney Oldfield won with the 999 in 1904. Henry Ford understood that racing helped improve the breed and sell cars. So it was a shock when Ford Motor Company pulled out of official factory-backed competition in 1970. By 1980, Ford had nothing that could compare with the Camaro. When the powers that be in Dearborn decided to chase the checkered flag again in 1981, they approached Michael Kranefuss, a German involved with the Zakspeed Capris in Europe. Ford brought together a group of experts in their fields, such as engineering, marketing, designers, and others to form Special Vehicle Operations (SVO). Kranefuss was at the helm.

SVO spearheaded Ford's return to racing with factory involvement. It was also responsible for getting high-performance parts into the hands of enthusiasts. But the biggest job was to develop a street production car that would take advantage of Ford's racing prowess. The money raised from the sales of these vehicles would fund Ford's racing activities.

Soon SVO was showing its flag on a wide spectrum of racing venues, and the street car was being shaped. The decision was made to create a grand touring car, a vehicle that could slice through curves with the best. As Randy Leffingwell writes in his book *Mustang*, "Ford already had a car to burn rubber. It was already called a Mustang, a 5.0-liter H.O. There was no need to have two."

The Fox platform was still under the Mustang's body, tweaked each year in the name of stylistic freshness. But for the SVO Mustang, the tweaks turned into a serious twist. The conventional grille was eliminated, and the hood curved down in a bold sweep to a point a couple of inches above the bumper. The bulk of air needed for the engine came from under the bumper. A

From the mouse-hair dash panel to the short-throw shifter, the Mustang SVO's interior was designed for sport driving. Recaro-style seats and ample legroom meant that a comfortable position could be achieved easily.

From the rear quarter view, the SVO emblem was plain to see yet subtle and refined. The SVO provided stunning turbo performance in the finest handling Mustang of that time.

NACA scoop sat atop the hood and was slightly offset to the passenger side. At the rear was a polycarbonate spoiler, but quite unlike any seen on a Mustang before. This was a twin-deck arrangement that was composed of a conventional lower spoiler augmented by another full-sized spoiler mounted on the lower portion of the rear hatch glass. It provided more of a stylistic effect rather than generate downforce, but it was a dramatic sight. It did in fact produce negative rear lift, -0.011 lift versus +0.085 for a base Mustang.

A small displacement, high-output, lightweight engine was needed to provide the ideal weight balance and thus the superb handling characteristics Ford wanted to achieve. The 2.3-liter turbocharged engine was the powerplant chosen for the new Mustang, but first it would undergo some serious massaging. The 2.3 turbo engine had been installed in the 1983 Thunderbird Turbo Coupe, but without an intercooler. The version installed in the Mustang SVO produced significantly more horsepower.

To commemorate 15 years of model history, Ford released the 1984 Twentieth Anniversary Edition GT350. This rare and highly collectable car was available with a 175-horsepower 5.0 V-8 and (as pictured here) a 145-horsepower, 2.3-liter turbo four. Only 104 1984 Twentieth Anniversary Edition Turbo GT350 convertibles were built. A pricey option, the turbo convertible cost $13,441. This was the last Mustang to bear the GT350 name.

The turbo's compression ratio was 8.0:1, and the tuned-port Bosch/Ford fuel-injection system was now electronic. The iron block/head held a single overhead camshaft working hydraulic lifters. An intercooler was added, bringing the temperature of the air down from 300 degrees to 175 degrees as it exited the turbo and passed through the air-to-air heat exchanger. Horsepower rose to 175, peaking at 4,400 rpm, and redline came in at 6,100. Torque was rated at 210 foot-pounds at a lofty 3,000 rpm. The small

four-banger produced little low-end torque until the Garrett AiResearch T-3 turbo produced significant manifold pressure. A two-position switch mounted on the center console allowed the use of premium and lower octane fuel. Typically, the turbo would deliver up to 14-psi boost, but the low octane setting would limit boost to 10-psi. Unlike the Thunderbird turbo that used a mechanical control of the boost, the SVO used the EEC-IV electronic engine control system that regulated boost, engine timing, engine idle rpm, exhaust gas recirculation, and the Thermactor emission control system. Superior fuel economy was one of the advantages to having a small displacement engine. The EPA rated the SVO at 21 miles per gallon for city driving and 32 miles per gallon on the highway; that had to help the CAFE numbers. Another plus was the SVO's weight distribution; the front/rear numbers of 56.6/43.4 percent helped the GT car to deliver a balanced ride.

But the engine was not the only area where the gang at SVO had worked their magic. The vehicle/ground interface was worked over to turn the Mustang SVO into the finest road pony car that Ford had built to that date. Better, truer steering was a goal, as was a ride that, while it would cling to the road like a leech, would not rearrange your internal organs. The engineers started with the front suspension, replacing the stock stamped lower control arms with the forged units from the

The hood scoop was fitted to clear the engine with the bottom of the hood, not to act as a functional air inlet. The GT350 received numerous suspension enhancements, such as a modified MacPherson strut front suspension with an antiroll bar, and a four-link rear axle with special coil springs and gas-filled shock absorbers.

Lincoln Continental. Attached to them were three-way adjustable Koni shock absorbers. The front coil springs, as well as the bushings, were specially developed for this application. The front antisway bar had a diameter of 1.20 inches, and all of the modifications resulted in a 1-inch lower ride height. Rack-and-pinion steering gave a direct feel between the front tires and the leather-wrapped three-spoked steering wheel.

A live rear axle had its motions controlled with a four-link setup. Coil springs were used, as well as the adjustable Koni shocks. Cast-aluminum 16x7-inch wheels were wrapped in Goodyear 225/50VR16 BSW NCTs. This metric tire was used because the 1984 Corvette used the Goodyear Gatorback tire that Ford wanted to use. But Chevrolet and Goodyear had signed an agreement that prevented the Gatorback to be used on anything but the 'Vette. Goodyear did have this tire from Germany in the system though. . . .

The brakes were noteworthy, as this was the first time that four-wheel discs were installed on the Mustang from the factory. Fitted with ventilated 10.9x1.1-inch rotors on the front and ventilated 11.3x0.9-inch at the rear, they brought the SVO to a halt in 217 feet in the October 1983 *Car and Driver* test. The rear rotors were larger than the fronts due to the need for a parking brake that would pass the government test. In order for the brake to hold the vehicle on a hill after cooling for 30 minutes, the mass of a larger rotor was necessary.

But the Mustang SVO was made for moving, not for being parked. The staff at *Car and Driver* flogged the newest pony car in its October 1983 issue, and the results spoke well of Ford's efforts. The best 0-to-60-mile-per-hour run netted a time of 7.5 seconds. *Motor Trend*, 10/83, took a little longer to get to 60 miles per hour. It took 8.12 seconds. The quarter-mile was seen in the mirrors after 16.08 seconds, tripping the lights at

80

86.0 miles per hour. Top speed was a whisker under 135 miles per hour, the Traction-Lok limited-slip 3.45:1 rear axle ratio working to provide quick take-offs rather than top speed. The five-speed Borg-Warner T5 transmission was controlled with a short-throw Hurst shifter, the gearbox requiring a firm hand to slam it into the next gear. But at least you knew the power was going in the right direction.

A comfortably equipped Mustang SVO would set a buyer back $15,585. That was serious coin for a vehicle that performed in a straight line as well as the 5.0-liter. The price might have had something to do with the sales of only 4,508 SVOs in 1984. But the SVO was never meant to tackle the big boys from stoplight to stoplight. It performed superbly on tight, twisting rivers of road. Then the Mustang and driver worked together, putting tarmac behind and smiles on the face. The SVO showed that Ford was very serious in putting capable road machines into production. And serious about raising expectations about what to expect from a pony car.

## TWENTIETH ANNIVERSARY EDITION GT350 MUSTANG

Many vehicles have a lifespan of less than half a dozen years before they're consigned to a footnote in automotive history. Any automobile that has seen 15 years of service must be doing something right. For both the automobile manufacturer as well as loyal customer, 20 years of model history is a milestone. So it was with proud fanfare that Ford celebrated the platinum birthday of the original pony car.

Long before 1984, Ford had been at work to inject power and agility into the Fox platform's sporty offering. The 5.0-liter engine was steadily gaining horsepower each year as the engineers

used electronics to reduce emissions and improve fuel economy and durability. The manufacturers were pushing small displacement turbocharged engines over naturally aspirated V-8s of yesteryear. In this vein, the SVO was released in 1984, complete with an intercooled four-cylinder mill that pumped out 175 horsepower. But Ford saw that the demand for the V-8 was alive and well. The company's small-block engine put out 205 horses, and it cost less than the high-tech SVO. So when plans were drawn up to celebrate the 20th anniversary of the Mustang, it was decided to offer two different powerplants to the customer and see what would sell.

The 5.0-liter HO (High Output) V-8 was slipped under the hoods of the vast majority of the Oxford White/Canyon Red Mustang GTs. This faithful engine enjoyed the same types of tweaks to extract power that worked in the good old days. The 90-degree V-8 had the same bore and stroke of 4.00 by 3.00 inches as the Boss 302, and it had an 8.3:1 compression ratio. The valves were actuated by hydraulic lifters. A Holley four-barrel 4180C carburetor, rated at 600 cfm, handled the fuel/air mixture. A five-speed Borg-Warner T-5 manual overdrive transmission took care of gear changes. Its 175 peak horsepower was produced at 4,000 rpm, and 245 foot-pounds of torque were delivered at 2,200 revs.

The second powerplant offered was the 2.3-liter turbocharged inline four-cylinder engine. But unlike the SVO, this engine was not fitted with an intercooler. Consequently, output was not quite on a par with the SVO version. Called the Turbo GT, the little engine had a compression ratio of 8.0:1 and a bore and stroke of 3.781 by 3.126 inches. Electronic fuel injection was standard. Maximum power was 145 horsepower at 4,600 rpm, and torque was rated at 180 foot-pounds at 3,600 rpm.

The fuel-injected Turbo GT had a compression ratio of 8.0:1 and a bore and stroke of 3.781 by 3.126 inches. Maximum power was 145 horsepower at 4,600 rpm, and torque was rated at 180 foot-pounds at 3,600 rpm. The 2.3-liter motor housed 3.45:1 gears in the differential.

This level of performance wouldn't melt the sticky P220/55R390 Michelin TRX tires. Standard rear-axle ratios were 3.08:1 for V-8-equipped Anniversary Editions, while the 2.3-liter motor housed 3.45:1 gears in the differential.

Midway through the model year, Ford introduced another version of the trusty 5.0-liter V-8. This came with central fuel injection (throttle body) and a four-speed automatic overdrive transmission. Output was 165 horsepower, while the rear axle ratio was 3.27:1.

Based on the GT package, the GT350 received all of the suspension goodies, such as a modified MacPherson strut front suspension with an antiroll bar and a four-link rear axle with special coil springs and gas-filled shock absorbers at each corner. An air dam was installed and road lamps were available. Brakes were the disc/drum combo that saved Ford money.

The anniversary package was sold for both three-door hatchback and convertible. Running the length of the lower sill area between the front and rear tires was the same GT350 script and striping that appeared on the famed Shelbys of the mid-1960s. While Ford had purchased the rights from Shelby to put on the Cobra name, it had not received permission to use the GT350 or GT500 logos. So it was no surprise lawyers representing Carroll Shelby took legal action to stop Ford from using the GT350 name.

Production of the 20th Anniversary Edition GT350 Mustangs was completed in 35 days of production, from March 5, 1984, to April 1984. When a customer bought an Anniversary Edition Mustang, it had a horseshoe emblem on the dash as delivered from the dealer. A few months after it was purchased, the owner would receive a card from Ford asking for information. After sending that card back, the owner would get another medallion in the mail, with a serial number and the owner's

A machined look was the style in Detroit in the mid-1980s. While the mandated 85-mile-per-hour speedometer was used, the car easily exceeded that high mark. More controls were being mounted on stalks, making it easier for the driver to control secondary functions.

name on it. It was to be mounted by the owner on the dash. It was a bit of flash that Ford hoped would turn the Anniversary Edition into a collector's item. Pricing ranged from $9,774 for a 5.0-liter three-door to $13,441 for a 2.3-liter Mustang GT Turbo convertible.

They sold well, with 5,260 units finding homes. All but about 500 units were equipped with the 5.0-liter V-8 powerplant, the surge of torque irresistible. And that was what Ford wanted to see, its 20-year-old all grown up and welcome in the world. While Ford used the Anniversary Edition as a marketing pitch, the Mustang would not have celebrated its 20th if it were not a sound vehicle. The public has a tendency to weed out the mediocre and reward the worthy. The Mustang had proved that it was more than worthy.

## CHAPTER FIVE

## HIGH PERFORMANCE REVISITED

The pendulum was swinging. During the early 1980s, Ford power had started to find its way under the Mustang's hood. Engineers were using new technology to restore the horsepower that Washington, D.C., had stripped away in the desire for cleaner air. The public had been clamoring for the return of serious, affordable performance. Detroit wanted nothing more than to fulfill the desires of potential buyers.

Ford had walked the path to power using a turbocharger, and did so to good effect. But the cost proved to be prohibitive to many customers, and Americans have a deep-seated love of large displacement, high-torque V-8 engines. Soft sales doomed the SVO, while the trusty 5.0-liter pushrod V-8 soldiered on. The engineers found that using a "yestertech"

The 1987 Mustang GT 5.0 was definitely the right car at the right time. Beyond a shadow of a doubt, Ford had returned to the high-performance game. Competition between Chevrolet's Camaro Z28 and the GT was inevitable. Tautly styled, well engineered, aggressively priced, these were unbeatable ingredients that Ford combined to make the 1987 GT the top pony car of its day. The GT hatchback option started at $12,106.

The Mustang GT was more than a match for most high-performance opposition on the street in the late 1980s. Most musclecars in the late 1980s left the Mustang alone that had the GT emblem on its flank. If a buyer wanted the V-8 but did not want the GT option, the engine alone cost $1,885. It was money well spent.

engine to supply the Mustang with large amounts of motivation was far easier and cheaper. And let's not forget that the public loved it.

The use of engine management computer systems made the return of high-performance inevitable. Increased power, improved mileage, and reduced emissions were the result of many years in engineering laboratories. When the old tire-smoking, musclecar-type performance re-emerged in the guise of the 5.0-liter GT, it caused a sensation. Affordable, attractive, and fast, everyone (except Camaro and Trans-Am drivers) wanted one. It helped the corporate bottom line at a time when it needed help. It put a Mustang into garages where a Mustang hadn't been in a decade. It showed that Ford was really listening to its customers. And it started a performance renaissance that continues to this day.

Now in the beginning of a new century, the Camaro/Firebird teeters on the edge of extinction while the Mustang flourishes. Ford has regained its perspective on the position of the Mustang in the marketplace and virtually has the segment to itself. The company knows better than to tamper with a winning formula. Ford has been there, done that. Yet the current Mustang is a credit to the team that dreamed up the original pony car so many years ago.

## THE 1987 MUSTANG 5.0

Every once and a while, all the planets line up in the automotive universe, and a vehicle is produced that combines performance, price, and value into an unbeatable package. The 1987 Mustang GT 5.0-liter was one such car, a fast, agile, good-looking machine that didn't break the bank, but could scare the hell out of the unwary. It was a superb-handling modern musclecar equipped with superb brakes, and the public loved it. The GT's performance made comparisons between it and cross-town rival Chevrolet's Camaro inevitable. While evenly matched on the track, the bottom line meant the Mustang buyer had a nice chunk of change left over. Easy on the eye, easy on the wallet–Ford's revitalized pony car was enjoying a renaissance. It ended up being better than its predecessors. The only losers were those driving other makes of vehicles.

In period ad copy for the Mustang GT, the following prose appeared: "The only excuse for changing the Mustang GT was to make a better Mustang GT." This was one instance when fact supported the advertising claim. Significant changes from 1986 turned the GT into a well-dressed street brawler. Between stylistic changes and an infusion of horsepower, the Mustang GT for 1987 was a much-improved version of the classic musclecar but with few of the vices. The

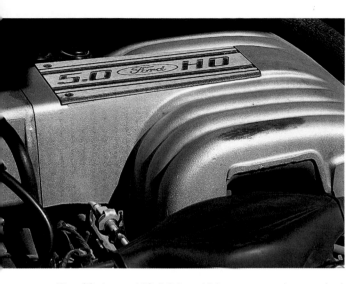

The 90-degree V-8 5.0-liter high-output engine cranked out 225 horsepower and 300 foot-pounds of torque. The fuel-injected engine filled the air with the wonderful American V-8 burble, and it could push the car to 150 miles per hour.

Mustang still rode on a 100.5-inch wheelbase, but the long hood gave it a longer look. With the departure of the SVO Mustang from the arena at the end of 1986, the GT was the sole high-performance Mustang and the recipient of Dearborn's engineering prowess. That meant this was a Mustang to remember.

Mustang GTs were available in two body configurations: a two-door hatchback and a convertible. At first glance, changes were evident, from the grille-less front to the louvered taillights. The sloping curve of the SVO grille down onto the front bumper was transferred to the GT, resulting in better aerodynamics as well as cleaning up the front. Flush-mounted halogen headlamps and fog lamps flanked the air inlet in the air dam. Faux air scoops were installed in front of each wheel, while lower sill moldings

gave the appearance of ground effects. The rear treatment elicited a love-it or leave-it attitude. Since the late 1940s, hot-rodders had used louvers as an engine cooling aid or a stylistic statement. The 1987 Mustang GT used a louvered look for the back lens. While the overall effect was questionable, there was never any doubt that you were following a 1986 model. A rear spoiler ran the width of the trunk's aft edge. Ford claimed it reduced the rear-end lift while raising the vehicle's aggressive appearance.

The interior was revised as well, with a two-spoke tilt steering wheel and six large, easy-to-read circular gauges, including a 7,000-rpm tachometer and a laughably inadequate 85-mile-per-hour speedometer. The front seats had power lumbar support, as well as lower thigh bolsters that slid out from the lower cushion. The meaty shifter fell easily to hand. The standard five-speed manual transmission slotted into the next gear with a satisfying feel. A four-speed, overdrive automatic transmis-

Louvered taillights were a stylistic touch that most people either loved of hated. Regardless of your leanings, there was no mistaking the Mustang at night for any other vehicle. The functional bumpers were nicely integrated into the overall design.

The inadequate speedometer could be buried at will. The Mustang GT was so popular, some police departments took to driving the fleet Mustang in order to catch speeders driving Mustangs. If you can't beat 'em . . .

sion provided consistent, reliable performance. The rear axle ratio with the five-speed was 2.73:1, and an automatic transmission-equipped car had a 3.08:1 set of gears at the other end of the driveshaft.

Suspension and steering were upgraded as well. The front tires were controlled by a power-assisted rack-and-pinion steering using a 14.7:1 steering ratio, which required 2.2 turns of the steering wheel to go from lock to lock. Front suspension components were modified MacPherson nitrogen-filled struts, variable-rate coil springs, and a 1.3-inch antisway bar. The SVO Mustang parts bin was raided, with the plastic ball joints and retuned bushings bolted to the bottom of the 1987 GT. More caster was dialed in, and the camber settings were massaged. The latter SVO Mustangs featured an improved rear suspension,

and it was installed on the GT model. The rear live axle was held in position with a four-link arrangement, a .82-inch antisway bar, and the Quadra-shock setup. This was a pair of nitrogen-filled shock absorbers in the normal staggered configuration as well a pair of Freon-filled shocks in a horizontal plane, designed to minimize wheel hop and maximize control.

Brakes were upgraded, as decreasing velocity is as important as gathering it. The GT was fitted with the 10.9-inch front disc brake rotors used on the Lincoln Continental sedan. The rear drums measured 9.0 by 1.8 inches and were one of the ways that Ford could aggressively price the Mustang below its competition. Stopping distances were good for pre-ABS days, 80 to 0 was achieved in 289 feet. Bolted next to the brakes were cast alloy 15 by 7-inch wheels, surrounded by Goodyear Eagle VR60 P225/60VR-15 Gatorbacks. These high-performance street tires used a tread pattern directly drawn from Goodyear's racing rain tire and were a significant reason for the Mustang GT handling as well as it did. On *Road & Track*'s 700-slalom test, the 'Stang threaded the cones at 63.6 miles per hour, while the lateral acceleration of 0.80 g-forces would pin a passenger against the door panel.

The biggest news for the Mustang GT in 1987 was the component that provided rotational energy for the driveshaft. The 90-degree, 5.0-liter V-8 had the same bore and stroke—4.00 by 3.00 inches. It used five main crankshaft bearings, but

**Right**
Created by Ford's Special Vehicle Team, the 2000 Cobra R is a full-tilt production race car. It is the modern version of the original Shelby GT350, except that the Cobra R is only available in red and was sold only at Ford showrooms. One of the sweetest musclecars I've ever driven.

compression had been raised a bit to 9.2:1. Forged pistons with a .030-inch dish filled the cylinders. Revised cylinder heads, sourced from the pre-1986 5.0-liter truck engine, provided much improved flow. More fuel was inducted into the engine. A larger 60-millimeter throttle body, rated at 622 cfm, and larger capacity injectors were used on the sequential multiport fuel-injection system. The larger fuel mixers could stuff 19 pounds of fuel per hour in the engine system. Roller tappets and roller rocker arms were carried over from the previous year. The tubular exhaust manifolds used 2.25-inch tubing, and the exhaust system's H-pipe flowed back through the dual catalysts to the true dual exhaust.

The result of all these mechanical changes? More of everything performance buyers wanted. Horsepower was rated at 225 at 4,400 rpm, and torque weighed in with 300 foot-pounds at 3,000 rpm. Performance was on a par with the Chevrolet Camaro IROC-Z, equipped with essentially an iron-head version of the 350-ci Corvette engine. The Bowtie competition offered 220 ponies at 4,200 rpm, with a torque reading of 320 foot-pounds at 3,200 revs. So the classic Ford versus Chevy grudge match was alive and well.

The 3,160-pound Mustang GT generated impressive performance numbers. Magazine tests of the day showed that the GT had become a wicked barn burner. In the October 1986 issue of *Road & Track*, the Mustang GT went head-to-head against the Camaro IROC-Z. The rivals showed remarkable similarities. The Chevy was more expensive and emphasized the all-out performance approach, that is, maximum acceleration. Ford took a more user-friendly tack–a smoother ride and a quieter cabin. But don't think for a moment that the Mustang took a back

The lineage between these two vehicles is clear and unmistakable. The Mustang has stayed true to its roots, though today's Cobra R can lay claim to the most expensive production Mustang of all time at $55,000.

seat. The GT ran the quarter-mile in *exactly* the same amount of time as the Camaro–15.3 seconds. The Mustang was faster across the line at 93.0 miles per hour, however, while the Camaro measured 90.5. The two rivals' top speeds were separated by 1 mile per hour. The GT ran flat out at 148 miles per hour, and the IROC-Z racked up 149 miles per hour. These velocities were in Supercar territory only a few years before, yet anyone with $12,548 could drive the Mustang GT into his or her garage.

Ford had found the formula for keeping the performance/pollution equation in balance. The EPA rated the Mustang GT at 16 miles per gallon in the city, but buyers didn't get this option package to scrimp at the pump. The GT could take a weekend trip in comfort, then kick butt at the strip or on the street. It was the right car at the right time. Ford had been toying with the idea of replacing the rear-drive Mustang with a front-drive platform, ala Ford Probe. But sales of the Mustang rose with each new injection of power. So the success of the Mustang GT went a long way toward the development of the SN-95 platform. Even today, the 1987 Mustang GT is a force to be reckoned with. It was a great car then, and it's a great car now.

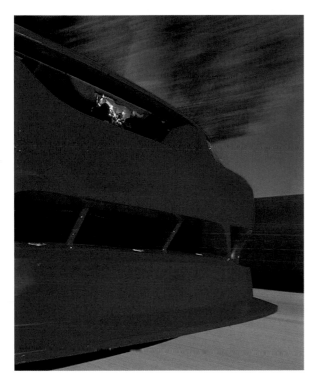

The splitter is a race-car–derived piece that can be removed for daily street use by twisting the Dzus fasteners and pulling the items away from the vehicle. While care must be exercised when driving on public streets with the functional splitter, it is mandatory for high-speed duty at a track. Drivers of the Cobra R get accustomed to the world passing by in a blur.

## THE 2000 SVT MUSTANG COBRA R

In 1989, Ford built a new Mustang to comply with downstream legislation. Increasingly stringent government regulations meant that vehicles needed to get improved mileage as well as reducing tailpipe emissions. The 1994 Mustang, using the FOX-4 platform, was an evolutionary improvement over the prior model. The GT model came with the MN-12 version of the 5.0-liter V-8 that had propelled Mustangs down so many roads. Rated at 215 horsepower at 4,200, and 285 foot-pounds of torque at 3,400 revs, the small block was carried over from 1993. But in 1993, Ford's Special Vehicle Team (SVT) descended from the SVO group to build the ultimate Mustang, a racing version of the production Cobra Mustang called the Cobra R. It was hard to believe the 240-horsepower Cobra wasn't enough, but this was a car built to beat the competition into submission on the SCCA road racing circuit.

So SVT whipped up the Cobra R. Buyers had to show a competition license and a desire to compete on a racetrack. Called the R, its name recalled the Shelby R-Model care cars from the mid-1960s. This new version was an all-Ford product and the last year of the Fox platform. Ford wanted it to go out with a bang.

Starting with the Mustang SVT Cobra, the Cobra R tossed everything that might be superfluous to getting across the finish line first. Missing components included air conditioning, power windows, fog lamps, inner-fender panels, and some of the sound insulation. Under the hood was a 5.0-liter V-8, mechanically no different from the standard Cobra 235-horsepower engine. Only 107 were built, and most went into collectors' hands rather than racers. But the ones that saw combat on the racetrack suffered from

This is one of the things the Cobra R does best, leaving souvenir black lines in its wake. The side-exiting exhaust fills the air with a glorious exhaust note, and the racetrack intent of the vehicle becomes clear when looking for the air conditioner controls—no such thing.

The 2000 Cobra R can use its 385 horsepower to propel itself to frightening top speeds. The Cobra R has recorded a 0-to-60-mile-per-hour time of 4.8 seconds, and a quarter-mile performance of 13.0 seconds, 108.5 miles per hour.

insufficient low-end torque, a small fuel tank, and inadequate brakes that faded badly. It was a clear sign that Ford and SVT were serious about high performance and re-establishing a presence in sports car racing.

With the release of the new body style in 1994, SVT ramped up to release another Cobra R in 1995. Once again, this was a low-volume race special. Only 250 were built. Engine size had increased to 351 ci, horsepower was rated at 300, and torque measured up at 365 foot-pounds. Built just for competition again, it sold out in days.

Fast forward to the new millennium. SVT released its third Cobra R, and it was a stormer from the word *go*. John Coletti, Ford Special Vehicle Engineering (SVE) manager, laid out the parameters for a Cobra R. "This is the kind of car you want to do, when it's time," he said. "We have a simple rule of thumb for when it's time to develop a new Cobra R: first, when there's a need, and second, when the new one will be able to far outshine the old one."

A 5.4-liter, DOHC V-8 from the Triton Modular engine family was selected. This tall engine featured a cast-iron block that used the same 90.2-millimeter bore as the 4.6-liter aluminum engine, but the stroke was increased from 90.0 to 105.8 millimeters. A forged steel crankshaft rests in Federal Mogul rod bearing, as well as Carrillo billet-steel connecting rods. The flat-topped, forged aluminum pistons increased wall and pin strength for high rpm use, and a 9.60:1 compression ratio was achieved.

On top of the block are the special four-valve cylinder heads, initially developed for Ford's off-road truck racing program. They have better than 25 percent more airflow than the 4.6-liter Cobra heads. The intake valves have a head diameter of 37 millimeters, and the exhaust valves have a 32-millimeter diameter. Another reason for the increased flow is the amount of valve lift, 13 millimeters for intake valves and 12 millimeters on the exhaust side. The throttle body is a single oval bore, with an 80-millimeter mass-air sensor. A low-restriction aluminum intake manifold handles the air distribution duties using tuned equal-length runners, while tubular stainless-steel, short-tube headers mate up with a Bassani X-pipe, then into regular production Cobra catalytic converters. Downstream are Borla mufflers and exhaust tips that exit in front of the rear tires.

The Cobra R develops 385 healthy horsepower at 6,250 rpm, and the torque measures 385 foot-pounds at 4,250 rpm. Like most DOHC engines, peak power comes on in the upper half of the rev range, and it comes on like a river unleashed. With a redline of 6,500 rpm, it does not take long for the tach's needle to swing into the danger zone when pushing the accelerator into the carpet. Engine overrevving is protected by 6,800 rpm fuel shut-off and an ignition cut-off kicks in at 7,000 rpm. The sound of this engine climbing to the next gear is gloriously habit-forming. No radio is installed; none is needed.

Connected to the aft end of the engine is a 11.0-inch, single-plate clutch, hooking up to a McLeod aluminum flywheel. For the first time in Mustang history, a six-speed manual transmission was installed, a Tremec T56 unit, with a 4-inch aluminum driveshaft connected to a 3.55:1 Gerodisc hydro-mechanical differential.

The suspension is up to the task of putting the power to the ground. Or at least making very long black lines. The front suspension is made up of a modified MacPherson strut with gas-charged Bilstein shocks, 800-pound Eibach springs, and a 28-millimeter tubular stabilizer bar. The camber causes the front tires to lean like road racing cars. The rear suspension is really a treat. For the first time, a Cobra R uses a dual A-arm independent setup. The upper arm is steel, and the lower control arm is aluminum. Four Bilstein gas-charged shocks and 750-pound-per-inch Eibach coil springs and a 26-millimeter tubular stabilizer bar keep the massive rubber in proper contact with the ground.

The rolling stock is the stuff dreams are made of. The Cobra R has five-spoke cast-aluminum wheels measuring 18 by 9.8 inches. They are teamed up with BF Goodrich g-Force KD 265/40ZR-18 tires, which are made of a custom compound made especially for the Cobra R.

Tucked inside of the huge wheels are huge brakes, capable of hauling the 3,590-pound license plate-able race car down from the go-directly-to-jail-speeds. Brembo four-piston caliper brakes equipped with Galpher pads and mated to front-vented, 13-inch Brembo discs provide the stopping power. Instead of fog lamps in the air dam, the removable splitter has functional brake cooling ducts feeding the air into Multimatic carbon-fiber heat shields. At the back of the vehicle, 11.65-inch vented discs use a single-piston caliper and Akebono pads. The entire system uses four-sensor, four-channel ABS to ensure that trips to the upper end of the 180-mile-per-hour speedometer have a happy ending.

The gang at *Motor Trend* took a Cobra R to Ford's Kingman, Arizona, proving grounds in August 2000 and recorded a 60-to-0-mile-per-hour distance of only 116 feet. Some of the other numbers they noted was a 0-to-60-mile-per-hour time of 4.8 seconds, and a quarter-mile performance of 13.0 seconds, 108.5 miles per hour. No doubt about it, these numbers are supercar numbers. Being behind the wheel can only be described as a blast. Recaro front seats hold the driver and one passenger firmly in place. There is no rear seat, just a carpeted open area, like a 1965 Shelby GT350. In front of the driver is a

The heart of the Cobra R is this iron-block 5.4-liter DOHC V-8, topped by a plenum so large that the hood had to be bulged to provide clearance. The aluminum intake manifold used tuned equal-length runners to ensure good flow up to the 6,500-rpm redline. The chain drive turned the exhaust cams, which then used a secondary chain to drive the intake cams. The roller finger followers used hydraulic lash adjustments to activate the ovate-wire, beehive-shaped valve springs.

complete set of white-faced gauges, the speedo's scale going to 180 miles per hour. The B&M Ripper shifter falls easily into the hand, and there is no doubt when the next gear is engaged. Rolling down city streets in search of prey, care must be given to the very low splitter trying to divide the air stream over and under the Cobra. With rubber this huge, the turning radius of 43 feet, 7 inches is not unusual. The view through the back window is surprisingly good, surprising because the 7-inch high rear spoiler does not block vision.

Only 300 2000 Cobra Rs were built, each one showing about $55,000 on the window sticker. They were available in any color, as long as it was Performance Red with a Dark Charcoal interior.

The Cobra R will plaster an ear-to-ear grin on your face faster than you can say "skid marks." The latest SVT Mustang Cobra R is far better than its predecessors. And just as rare. If you ever have the chance to get behind the wheel and scream down a lonely stretch of road, think of all the Mustangs that rolled down that road before and made the Cobra R a reality.

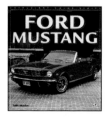
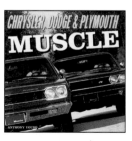